Copyright

Book cover design by Patricia Strickland
Book cover image:
  ©iStock.com/AUDINDesign AshDesign/Getty Images

Production coordinated by S.J. Wright

Published by Koratious Press. First edition.

ISBN-13: 978-0-615-92224-9
ISBN-10: 0-615-92224-4

INVESTING FOR THE REST OF US

How To Invest In Stocks Using Index Funds: Passive Investing Strategies Everyone Can Use

David L. Wright

To my wife, without whom nothing is possible.

Acknowledgements

I would like to thank those whose contributions made this book possible: Amy Wilmore, Marilyn Sandoval, and Stephen Tolbert as they (and many others like them) were my motivation for writing this book; Warren Buffett and Charlie Munger for their inspiration from afar; Jane McKnight of Koratious Press for her assistance in developing the content of the book, and for her editing expertise polishing the manuscript; Patricia Strickland for her graphic design sensibilities on the cover of the book.

About this Book

Investing isn't something that everyone thinks about. In fact, many people don't want to give their investments any thought at all. My friends, colleagues, and co-workers have always asked me where to invest; that's why I wrote this book.

This book is for:

- Both beginning investors and people who have been investing for many years.

- Anyone who wants to learn about passive investing.

- Seasoned investors looking for a new approach to investing.

- People who already have money invested in the stock market, but don't really know where to invest their money.

- Those people who know that they should start to invest and save for their retirement but aren't sure what approach they should take to investing.

- People in a transitional state of employment. For instance, people who are moving their money from a 401(k) retirement plan from a previous employer to an IRA account and need to select the invest options for that IRA account.

Disclaimer

Most people gloss right over this part of a book. I know I usually do, so although I have to make the requisite disclaimers, I have also tried to put some interesting stuff in here as well.

First of all, I am not an investment advisor, and I do not engage in the business of advising others as to the advisability of investing in, purchasing, or selling securities. Nor am I in the business of issuing or promulgating analyses or reports concerning securities. My background is discussed in the About the Author Section, where I explain that my career has been spent largely as a Chief Financial Officer, and my investing experience has been for my own account.

Rather, I am the author (under my pseudonym, David L. Wright) and publisher of a line of digital publications (including this book, a related software application, spreadsheets, and a website located at DollarBits.com) where I share my own ideas and opinions about personal finance in general. These publications do not offer individualized or personalized advice attuned to any specific portfolio or to any reader's or users particular needs.

The information and advice in these publications should be viewed for general informational purposes only. As author and publisher, I make no assurances or predictions of success or failure as a result of the reader's or user's decision to make use of the ideas and opinions offered in these publications. As with all investment decisions, past performance is no guarantee of future results.

Quotations, screenshots and other material from third-party websites and other third-party sources that appear in these publications are used under the Fair Use Doctrine. All trademarks, copyrights and other intellectual property that may be included in these publications are the property of their respective owners.

The characterizations that you find in these publications regarding various third parties — such as, by way of example, brokerage houses, investment advisors, investment funds, investment portfolios, and the authors of other publications — are the opinion of the author and are based on facts that were believed to be accurate at the time of initial publication of these publications. None of the individuals, companies or other entities mentioned in these publications have sponsored or endorsed me or my publications in any way, and there is no affiliation of any kind between us.

Several times in my publications I refer to how much money can be made via certain products, methods, and/or strategies. In 2010, the US Federal Trade Commission (FTC) came out with a new law that indicates that if I state how much money I have or someone else has made using these methods, then I have to disclose the average income of everyone who has tried this. As you can imagine, I would have no way of finding that out. I would have to get annual income statements from all of the people who have read this book and acted upon it. But nevertheless, the FTC requires that I state the average. So here goes: I estimate the average person who buys this book and uses the methods herein earns on average something less than one cent.

Now here are some more disclaimers my lawyers insisted on. (If you wonder why these books are so expensive it's because we authors have to pay lawyers to read them!)

The purchaser, reader, and/or user of my publications assumes all responsibility for his or her decision to use the information and advice in these publications. Adherence to all applicable laws and regulations, including international, federal, state, and local governing professional licensing, business practices, advertising, and all other aspects of doing business in any jurisdiction is the sole responsibility of the purchaser, reader, and/or user.

Except as an independent seller, the author and publisher are not affiliated with any companies or websites that are mentioned within these pages, and we do not guarantee the performance or effectiveness of said websites.

Neither the author nor publisher assume any responsibility or liability whatsoever on behalf of any purchaser, reader, or user of these materials. No express or implied guarantees or predictions of any kind whatsoever, including the income that may or may not result from use of these materials, are made by the author and/or publisher.

All websites and URLs mentioned in this book were current at the time of initial publication. However, websites are often modified or removed, and URLs changed. The author and publisher are not responsible for any content on any website mentioned in this book other than their own.

Okay, that's it for the legal mumbo jumbo. Let's get started with the book.

Table of Contents

Chapter 1: It's Good to Be Passive

"Investing should be dull, like watching paint dry or grass grow. If you want excitement, take $800 and go to Las Vegas. It is not easy to get rich in Las Vegas, at Churchill Downs, or at the local Merrill Lynch office."

~ Paul Samuelson (First Nobel Prize Winner, Economics, 1970)

Has anyone ever called you dull or passive? It usually doesn't feel good when someone suggests that you are a dull or passive person. These words have an almost universally negative connotation. However, when it comes to investing, being passive may be the easiest way to becoming a millionaire. Read that again... it may not be the quickest way, but it might well be the easiest way, short of winning the lottery or inheriting a million dollars from a long lost relative! Over the following pages, I will teach you an easy way to become a disciplined, passive investor.

Many beginning investors are drawn to the glamour of the stock market. They want the excitement of buying and selling shares in today's hot new company; some even get addicted to the excitement of trying to outperform the stock market. Paul Samuelson, a Nobel Prize Winner in Economics, is quoted as saying that most people would be better off being characterized as dull investors, and leaving their portfolios alone, as opposed to tinkering with them by buying and selling investments in their accounts.

That's an excellent suggestion. Most folks would be much better off taking a passive approach to investing by just making a few investment selections and then leaving them alone and allowing them to grow year-after-year, uninterrupted. But most people lack the discipline to be a passive investor.

In this short book, I am going to explain passive investing to you, and present you with examples of model portfolios which you may want to implement as your own investment portfolio. This is a different approach to investing than buying and selling stocks and/or mutual funds on a regular basis.

Most people buy and sell stocks, bonds, and mutual funds far too frequently. They will often sell their current investments and buy the investment vehicles which have most recently been outperforming the market or those which are being promoted as the next hot prospect. They get stock tips from friends, investment gurus on television, or their stock broker. They hear the latest investing advice, and then they sell their existing stocks to buy into that strategy. Brokers are motivated to entice their clients to trade more, thereby earning additional commissions, and most people are looking for a hot stock pick. It all results in trading that is usually too frequent and unsuccessful.

More often than not, most of us are simply better off being passive investors. But what is a passive investor? A passive investor selects one particular tried-and-true investment strategy and allows time and compounding to create wealth for him or her. A passive investor will invest his or her money into a small handful of investment products and allow the money to grow (based on historical norms), mostly on cruise control. Over the long haul, the passive investing portfolios recommended in this book have performed very well. These portfolios are typically comprised of index mutual funds, more commonly referred to as index funds.

What is an Index Fund?

Before I explain what an index fund is, I need to explain what an index is. A stock market index is a means by which a sector of the stock market is valued (i.e. Transportation Stocks, Utility Stocks, and Technology Stocks). Basically, an index fund is just a collection of stocks within a particular index (also sometimes referred to as a sector). For instance, the S&P 500 is an index which is comprised of 500 of the largest USA-based publicly traded companies. An S&P 500 index fund is usually comprised of all of the stocks which make up the S&P 500 index, weighted by their size. In general, an index fund is a group of selected stocks which seeks to mimic the movement of the particular index to which it is related. This fund can be a subset of the companies in that index, or all of them, depending on the fund's directive.

Index funds are one type of mutual fund. Mutual funds are a collection of investments that are pooled together. In the broadest sense, there are two types of mutual funds: actively managed funds, and passively managed funds. Index funds, for the most part, are passive investment vehicles. Managed funds are, as their name implies, actively managed funds. Managed funds have one or more fund managers who guide the performance of their fund by buying and selling investment vehicles (like stocks, bonds, other mutual funds, etc.). Fund managers have the ability to assess the current market situation and adjust their investments accordingly. That is, if the fund managers think a particular stock is overvalued, they may choose to sell that stock. Likewise, if the fund managers think a particular stock is undervalued, they can invest in that stock as they deem appropriate.

Index fund managers typically do not have this freedom to buy or sell stocks as they see fit. Index funds are not really managed. The people who run these funds tend to not make changes to their fund's portfolios based upon a stock's current valuation, various market conditions, or their opinions as to the stock market's future direction. For the most part, the role of an index fund manager is rather passive. (We like passive!)

Most index fund managers simply use a strategy whereby they have an investment in each and every security (stocks, bonds, etc.) in their index fund's benchmark, in the same weighting as that benchmark. For example, the manager of an S&P 500 index fund will likely just buy all of the stocks which comprise the S&P 500 in the same weighting in which the S&P 500 weights those stocks. Occasionally, a stock will be removed from the S&P 500 and replaced by another stock. On that rare occasion, the S&P 500 index fund manager might simply sell all of the shares of the outgoing stock and use the proceeds from that sale to buy an appropriate number of shares of the incoming stock.

> *The S&P 500 is one of the most closely followed indices in the world today. Perhaps the only index that is more closely watched would be the Dow Jones Industrial Average (commonly referred to as "The Dow"). If you would like to learn more about the S&P 500 index (i.e. its historic performance, its selection criteria, etc.), you can visit Standard & Poors' directly at their website: http://us.spindices.com/indices/equity/sp-500*

Logic would dictate that managed funds would outperform index funds. After all, the people who run managed funds can react to economic news and reports of any impending financial crises. These fund managers can sell the stocks that they think are due to decrease in value whenever they want to, and buy stocks that they think are undervalued and will be excellent investments in the future. Conversely, an index fund manager's charter would likely require him or her to "stay the course" and not make any changes to his or her fund.

So which of these funds performs better: managed funds where the fund managers get to buy and sell stocks as they deem appropriate, or passive funds where the fund managers typically don't make any changes to their fund's portfolio? Although it might seem counterintuitive, historical data has shown that most managed funds do NOT outperform index funds. (As a reminder, most index funds are passively managed.) Index funds have outperformed 80% of all mutual funds that are run by professional investment managers. Four out of five actively managed mutual funds have underperformed their associated index. Therefore, unless you are lucky enough to select the one-out-of-five actively managed funds which outperform their associated index, you are probably much better off investing in index funds than you would be by investing in managed funds.

Passively managed portfolios are typically comprised of a group of index funds. It is possible to outperform passively managed portfolios, but unless you plan on monitoring your investment portfolio all the time, or are fortunate enough to select one of the fund managers that consistently beats the market, my best recommendation to you is that you adopt a passive investing strategy and construct a portfolio comprised of index funds. The odds certainly favor this approach.

Most of us don't have the time, inclination, or skills to closely monitor our portfolios. As such, we are generally much better off leaving our investments alone rather than making frequent changes. Most investors are better off creating a passively managed portfolio which is basically a "set-it-and-forget-it" strategy.

Over the next few pages, I will present several passively managed portfolio options. These portfolios are not complex. In fact the investment plan-of-action for a passive portfolio is incredibly simple. You buy shares in the suggested proportions of each of several index funds. Then occasionally, perhaps once each year or so, you rebalance your portfolio to bring the balances back to their suggested proportions. (We'll discuss rebalancing in Chapter 7.) "Set-it-and-forget-it." Well, it's not quite that simple, it's more like "set it and readjust it once a year." Still, it's simple enough... Okay, let's get started!

Chapter 2: Churning is for Butter

> "Wall Street is the only place that people ride to in a Rolls Royce to get advice from those who take the subway."
>
> ~ Warren Buffett (American business magnate, and widely considered the most successful investor of the 20th century.)

A passively managed portfolio doesn't sound very exciting. You buy a few index funds and then essentially ignore them... Where's the fun in that? Most people want excitement in their lives. When it comes to their investments, they want to buy the next hot stock and see the value of their portfolio increase dramatically. Over the years, there have been many hot stocks which have had incredible gains. Let's look at the performance of a few stocks during the 1990's. If you had the opportunity to invest $1,000 in Apple, Microsoft, or Dell back in 1990, you would have done quite well for yourself. But you might be surprised to learn which of these three stocks performed best... A $1,000 investment in Apple at the start of 1990 would have been worth almost $3,000 by the end of 1999. That's a very nice return. Had you purchased Microsoft's stock, you would have done much better. If you owned Microsoft's stock throughout the 1990's, your $1,000 investment would have grown to more than $94,000. However, an investment in Dell would have done even better – a lot better. Had you owned Dell throughout the 1990's, your $1,000 investment would have been worth an incredible $822,000 at the end of 1999! (The performance achieved by Dell and Microsoft in the 1990's was phenomenal. Investors should not expect these types of returns.)

So now let's do the same thing for the first decade of the 2000's. Let's assume it is January 2000. We survived the Y2K crisis and now we want to invest money in the stock market. We will assume that we did not invest in Apple, Microsoft, or Dell in the 1990's, and that we are starting out with $1,000. We will have the same opportunity as before. We can invest our $1,000 into Apple, Microsoft, or Dell. You may be surprised to learn what your investment would have returned.

Apple's stock did better in the 2000's than it did in the 1990's. A $1,000 investment in Apple in 2000 was worth over $7,500 by the end of 2009. Microsoft and Dell fared a little differently. Given what you knew in 2000, you might have been tempted to invest your money in Dell. After all, you could have turned $1,000 into more than $800,000 during the 1990's. However, past per-formance is no guarantee of future results. Had you purchased $1,000 of either Microsoft or Dell on the first trading day in 2000 and held that stock until the end of 2009, you would have achieved a less than stellar return. A $1,000 in-vestment in Microsoft would have been worth only $639, and if you had invested that $1,000 in Dell stock, it would have been worth just $282. Ouch! This is an excellent illustration as to why you would need to closely monitor your portfolio should you decide to invest in individual stocks.

There are many similar stories in the tech sector. Many of the top-performing technology companies in the 1990's were among the worst performing companies in the 2000's. For instance, a $1,000 investment in EMC (a computer storage company) in the 1990's grew to over $757,000! However, had you purchased EMC in 2000, it would have been worth just $313 by the end of 2009. Then there is JDS Uniphase Corporation. JDS designs and manufactures products for optical communications networks. They went public in late 1993. If you had invested $1,000 in JDS Uniphase when they went public, your investment would have grown to over $313,000 by the end of the 1990's! Had you waited to purchase shares of JDS until the beginning of 2000, your investment would have been worth just $10.97 by the end of 2009. Yes, you read that correctly. A $1,000 investment into JDS in 2000 was worth less than $11 by the end of 2009. This company is still in business today, but many other technology companies that were formed and went public in the 1990's have since gone out of business.

And it's not just in the technology sector that we see such wild swings. If you had purchased shares of Eastman Kodak or Enron and held on to them, you would have lost your entire investment. Investments in the New York Times, the Gannett Company (owners of USA Today), and the Washington Post would have resulted in profits in the 1990's. In the 2000's the New York Times and the Gannett Company both lost about two-thirds of their value, while the Washington Post "only" lost about 10% of its value.

While the technology sector ran into difficulty in the early 2000's, the financial sector had a tough time in the latter part of the 2000's. Let's assume that on the first trading day in the year 2000 you had elected to invest $1,000 into each of the following four banks: Wells Fargo, Bank of America, Citicorp, and Washington Mutual. At the end of 2009, your $1,000 investment in Wells Fargo would have been worth $1,845. That works out to be an approximate 6.3% annualized return on your investment. Not bad at all, especially when you consider the issues in the financial sector at that time. By the end of 2009, a $1,000 investment in Bank of America would have been worth about $940. So you would have basically broken even. Your hypothetical investment in Citicorp fared a lot worse however. At the end of 2009, that $1,000 investment in "Citi" would have been worth just $118. But the worst of these four bank investments would have been an investment into Washington Mutual. "WaMu" investors lost all of their money. WaMu wasn't the only bank to go "belly up." During the global financial crisis of 2007-2010, a total of 189 banks in the United States either went out of business or had their assets acquired by another financial institution.

These examples should illustrate for you just how difficult it is to try to select which stocks will perform well in the future. Past performance is no guarantee of future results; a very common thing to hear when researching investment vehicles.

Many investors invariably chase the best performing stocks, however the top performing stocks in one decade, can often turn out to be poor investments in the following decade. As an example, all of the 25 highest-performing stocks in the S&P 500 during the 1990's did worse in the 2000's. In fact, none of those 25 stocks finished in the top 150 stocks of the S&P 500 during the first decade of the 2000's.

Picking the next hot stock is clearly not easy, but many people want excitement from their investment portfolio and continue to try and find that next "winner." Consciously or otherwise, many people think of the stock market as a gambling casino. To use casino vernacular, first you "place your bet" on a company's stock. Let's use a fictitious company named XYZ, Inc. for our example. You "wager" on XYZ by purchasing its stock. Then you hope that XYZ's profits increase each and every year. You hope that there is considerable "buzz" about XYZ and that other investors recognize its value and as a result will bid up its stock price. However, there is no assurance that any of this will take place. In fact, the inverse can and often does occur. Over time, the price of XYZ's stock might actually be less than what you originally paid for it. So, as is the case in a casino, investing in stocks can result in loss. However, casino gambling is usually an all-or-nothing proposition. You place your wager. If you win, you collect your winnings. If you lose, you usually lose your entire wager. Losing in the stock market doesn't usually result in a total loss. Stock prices rarely go to zero, but they do fluctuate, and it is entirely possible that they will lose value and be below the price that you paid when you bought them.

Why do stocks lose their value? Shouldn't stock prices rise each and every year? After all, the costs of virtually all the goods and services you buy seem to go up every year. Shouldn't this result in increased profits for companies thereby resulting in higher valuations for their stock? Stock prices decline for a variety of reasons. Let's revisit XYZ, Inc. XYZ's profits might be erratic. If its profits are lower this year as compared to last year, even if it made money this year, investors might believe the value of XYZ is lower. As a result, those people who are considering buying XYZ might not be willing to pay as much for the stock as other investors did earlier.

Profits aren't the sole determining factor as to why stock prices rise or fall. There are many factors which impact a stock's price. XYZ might lose an important patent which might result in its losing a stranglehold on one of its key products, leading to a loss in revenue. XYZ's competition might gain market share and erode XYZ's market dominance. XYZ's main product might become obsolete. Or XYZ might temporarily fall out of favor with investors. These are just a few reasons why a company's stock price might decline. There are many different factors which influence the price of a company's stock.

The price of stocks can also be affected by external forces. For instance, the company's market sector (i.e. transportation) might be out of favor as a whole. Sometimes the price of an overwhelming majority of stocks might decline as a result of world events, as happened after the 9/11 terrorist attacks. The value that the market assigns to XYZ (and to every other publicly traded company) is based upon a variety of factors.

Today making investment decisions is much easier than it used to be. For decades, making investment decisions was extremely difficult. The vast majority of the information that was available about stocks was only easily accessible to those in the financial industry. If you wanted to buy or sell stocks, bonds, etc., you had to contact your full-service broker, usually by telephone or in-person. Your broker would offer suggestions about which stocks or bonds he or she felt were appropriate for you to buy or sell at that time. Then, with your approval, he or she would execute buy or sell orders for those investment options on your behalf, and you would be charged dearly (via commissions) for that advice, and for the order executions. The commissions for those buy or sell transactions were based upon the actual number of shares that were bought or sold, and could cost upwards of $100 per transaction. If you were to make a $5,000 investment and had to pay a $100 commission fee to execute that trade, your commission would cost you 2% for that trade. Therefore, the stock price would have to increase by 2% just for you to breakeven. Then when the time came for you to sell that investment, you would have to pay an additional commission, further eroding your returns.

Until May 1, 1975, stock brokerage commissions were at a set level used by all stockbrokers. On that date, the SEC (the Securities and Exchange Commission) deregulated the brokerage commissions for stock order executions. Prior to that date, a stock trade could easily cost hundreds of dollars in commissions. Afterwards discount brokers, like Charles Schwab, started offering discounted trade commissions. Stock trading commissions dropped to $50, then to $20. When stock trading moved online and various internet brokerage accounts became available in the late

1990's, commissions declined further to about $10 which is roughly where they are today.[1]

Getting advice and order executions from your stock broker was quite expensive. If your broker's recommendation proved accurate, you would likely make money. If your broker's recommendation was inaccurate for whatever reason, you would almost certainly lose money. Your broker might then recommend selling some portion of the investment vehicles (stocks, bonds, mutual funds, etc.) which you held in your portfolio and buying others to improve your portfolio's performance. This might work out well for you, but regardless, your broker would make money from the commissions on those transactions. So, while churning your portfolio (buying and selling stocks, bonds, mutual funds, etc.) frequently might have been profitable for your portfolio, it would definitely have been profitable for your broker. The more trades that you made, the more money your broker made. (This, in fact, still holds true today, even at the reduced commission schedules.)

---

1 http://sec.gov/news/speech/1975/111875loomis.pdf

With the advent of discount brokerage houses, most people no longer need to use full-service brokers to buy and sell stocks, bonds, mutual funds, and other investment products. Discount brokers typically charge about $10 per stock transaction, regardless of the number of shares that are being bought or sold. A $10 commission on a $5,000 stock transaction results in a 0.2% cost to place that stock order. So the stock price would only need to increase by 0.2% to get you back to breakeven. This cost advantage is just one of the reasons why I strongly advocate using a discount brokerage house.

Price isn't the only difference between discount brokers and full-service brokers. Remember I mentioned that full-service brokers would offer stock advice. Most discount brokers do not offer any investment advice; they just execute stock transactions on your behalf. So if you are going to invest with a discount broker, you are likely going to have to look elsewhere to get advice and recommendations about which stocks, bonds, and/or mutual funds to buy or sell.

In the past it may have been difficult to get information as to which companies to invest in, but that's certainly not the case today. Finding information about publicly traded companies is no longer a challenge for the average person. This information is readily available. In fact, there is arguably too much information available now. There are countless news and financial information sources, investing forums, personal financial blogs, etc., affording anyone the opportunity to get up-to-the-minute information and opinions about every publicly traded company.

Having all of this readily available information has certainly helped to level the playing field somewhat, allowing individuals to compete with professional stock traders. There is certainly no shortage of opinions. In fact, you would be hard-pressed to keep up with all the financial information that is published every single day. Financial websites, magazines, newspapers, radio and television shows are bombarding the investing public with opinions as to which stocks should be bought, held, or sold. A lot of the information is quite valuable and useful. Some of the information, well, not-so-much...

Many of the opinions being presented offer sound logical advice and can be quite convincing. When you combine all of this information with the fact that you can buy or sell stocks instantaneously and inexpensively on the internet, it is easy to see why people are tempted to churn their own portfolios. In some sense, you can't really blame them. The information and opinions offered can be quite compelling. It is incredibly easy to buy stocks by just accessing your account on the internet and clicking the "buy button," and it only costs you about $10 in commissions. It takes almost no effort to churn your portfolio.

We don't want to churn our portfolios. We don't want to buy and sell investment vehicles often in our accounts. Most of us are much better off owning index funds or similar investment vehicles, and only buying or selling when rebalancing or investing additional cash in our portfolios. Unless you are someone who is willing to put in the time and effort to closely monitor your portfolio on a very regular (think daily or weekly) basis, I strongly maintain that you would be much better off selecting one of the passively managed portfolios that I will discuss a little later in this book.

Chapter 3: Anatomy of a Passively Managed Portfolio

"A very low-cost index (fund) is going to beat a majority of the amateur-managed money or professionally-managed money funds..."

~ Warren Buffett

What is a passively managed portfolio? For that matter, what is a portfolio? A portfolio is simply the group of stocks, bonds, mutual funds, and/or other investment vehicles that you own. In some sense, a passively managed portfolio is aptly named because you simply buy your investment vehicles and leave them alone (more on all that in the subsequent chapters). There's a tiny bit more to it, which I will get into later as well, but it is basically a set-it-and-forget-it investment approach. Passively managed portfolios are made up of several investment vehicles, typically index mutual funds. As discussed in Chapter 1, we know that index funds are comprised of a group of stocks, bonds, or other investment vehicles, sometimes hundreds or thousands of them, in a particular investment category.

Passively managed portfolios are ideal for people who are either unwilling or unable to put in the time and effort that is truly necessary to monitor their portfolios. Monitoring your portfolio includes regularly reviewing financial reports and news stories about your investment vehicles, keeping current on economic trends, and trading as necessary, amongst other things. Most people don't have the time, the skills, the interest, or the inclination to monitor their portfolio closely enough to try to identify which investment options are undervalued and should be purchased or conversely, to identify and avoid an unanticipated negative impact to their portfolio and be able to determine when to sell an investment position. We all have better things to do with our time. Most of us are much better off utilizing a passive investing strategy.

If you want to buy individual stocks and bonds, you need to closely keep track of your portfolio's holdings. Unless you are buying the bluest of the blue chips – those companies which are considered to be incredibly safe investments – you will need to keep a very close eye on your investments so that you can act quickly and decisively to buy and/or sell your holdings as appropriate.

In fact, even the (presumably) safest stocks can fall precipitously. As mentioned in the previous chapter, Citicorp lost most of its value during the financial crisis of 2008. By March of 2009, Bank of America had also lost most of its value. These are two of the largest banks in the USA. They were considered to be among the safest investments available. During the last major financial crisis (when the "housing bubble" burst, between January 2007 and February 2009), these two gigantic financial institutions saw their stock prices decline by about 90%!

If you don't have the time or inclination to closely monitor your investment portfolio, I recommend that you avoid individual stocks and bonds altogether, and become a passive investor. I also recommend that you try to avoid actively managed mutual funds as well; however, this might not always be possible (I'll cover that in Chapter 14). For the passive investor, I recommend that you try to only invest in index funds. Why? Because: historically 80% of actively managed mutual funds underperform their corresponding index. That means that four-out-of-five actively managed mutual fund managers fail to perform as well as their associated index performs. Also, there are fees associated with mutual funds. The management fees that are associated with actively managed funds are almost always higher than they are for index funds (which are passively managed) – sometimes 10 or 20 times higher! This means you pay higher fees for the privilege of having an 80% chance of a lower return on your money. It just seems silly when it's spelled out that way, doesn't it?

Management fees are usually referred to as expense ratios. This is the amount of money that you pay for the fund manager to manage the fund's investments. The expense ratio is usually represented as a percent. (These fees are usually invisible to you as they are reflected in the price of the shares of the mutual fund. You can find the fees listed in the fund's prospectus, from your brokerage house, or from numerous financial websites such as Morningstar, Yahoo Finance, Google Finance, or MSN Money, just to name a few.)

The fees that are charged by passively managed index funds are much lower than the fees charged by actively managed funds. The justification for the higher fees for actively managed funds is that the fund managers are actively overseeing your investments for you. In 2013, the average fee for an actively managed stock mutual fund was 0.93% [2], that's ninety-three cents for every $100 invested. The average fee charged by passively managed index funds in 2013 was 0.13%. That's just thirteen cents for every $100 invested!

So why would you pay over seven times more in fees for actively managed investment mutual funds that (based on historical data) have an 80% likelihood of underperforming passively managed funds? I wouldn't, and neither should you.

---

2 Investment Company Institute: 2013 Investment Company Fact Sheet

Chapter 4: Passive Investing

"...at any given time, around a quarter of external managers will be outperforming their benchmarks, but the question is whether those managers that are doing well are canceled out by other managers that are underperforming..."

~ A CalPERS investment consultant as quoted in Pensions and Investment, March 2013

More and more investors of all sizes and types (individuals, corporations, government municipalities, etc.) are moving towards passive investing strategies. In fact, CalPERS, the second largest pension fund in the United States, is (at the time of this writing) in the process of switching to a passive investing strategy for its entire pension fund.

In Chapter 2, I talked about portfolio churning; how people receive advice (professional or other-wise) suggesting that they make changes to their portfolio based on current trends, news stories, investor speculation, or a wide variety of other whims and motivations. This advice usually spurs people on to trade in their accounts (chasing profits), but typically results in them only churn-ing their accounts and creating income for their brokers.

In Chapter 3, I explained the difference between actively managed mutual funds and passively managed index funds. The fund managers for actively managed mutual funds adjust their portfolios, buying and selling investments (stocks, bonds, etc.) as they deem appropriate. The management fees that are charged by actively managed funds are higher than those of index funds. Actively managed funds are much more likely to be churned than passively managed funds. In fact, some actively managed fund managers will sell and replace all of the stocks in their portfolio every single year. That's a lot of churning.

Index funds are much more passive, and partly because of this are able to charge lower management fees. By their charter, most index funds are usually required to essentially mimic the size and scope of the sector that they are trying to emulate. For instance, if an index fund is tasked with emulating the S&P 500, then that fund will be comprised of exactly those 500 stocks which make up that sector.

Basically, the only time that an S&P 500 index fund manager would buy or sell any of the stocks in his or her portfolio would be when there is a change to the make-up of the S&P 500. So when a stock is removed from the S&P 500 (for whatever reason) and is replaced by a new stock, the S&P 500 index fund manager would need to buy and sell stocks, to reflect those changes. Other than trading to reflect changes in their indices, most index funds remain pretty passive.

That's not to say that you can't churn a portfolio which is comprised of index funds by buying and selling them with some regularity. However, I do not recommend this behavior for a variety of reasons. As passive investors, it is not our goal to churn our accounts.

My recommendation is that you select a series of passively managed index funds with a pre-determined asset allocation [3] and make periodic adjustments to readjust your portfolio back to those original allocations. That's the passive investing strategy in a nutshell.

CalPERS (California Public Employees' Retirement Systems) is the second largest pension fund in the United States. They manage over $250 billion in retirement investments for many present and past employees of the State of California. They have been moving their quarter-of-a-trillion dollar investment portfolio away from actively managed investment vehicles to passively managed investments. In fact, as of this writing, CalPERS had more than half of their investment portfolio in passively managed index funds. They have indicated that they plan to have all of their investments in passively managed funds.

---

3 Asset allocation is an investment industry term meaning the apportionment of your investments by class. That is, the percentage of your investment dollars which you are putting into various investment categories (for instance: stocks, bonds, mutual funds, and cash).

If the second largest pension plan believes that passive investing is the fiscally responsible way to invest for its constituency, it's probably something that you should consider for your own investing strategy. In the next chapter, we will explore a few portfolios comprised of passively managed index funds.

Chapter 5: Passively Managed Portfolio Recommendations

Never invest in any idea you can't illustrate with a crayon.

~ Peter Lynch (Research consultant at Fidelity Investments)

Peter Lynch is a former mutual fund manager at Fidelity Investments. He has also written several extremely popular books on investing. His philosophy for the average investor is to keep it simple.

In Table 5.1, below, I've listed five fairly simple passive investment portfolios that many people are already using successfully, and that you may wish to consider for your personal portfolio. (I

have also included the S&P 500 index as a
benchmark.) Some of these have cute, clever
names like the Coffeehouse Portfolio or the
Margarita Portfolio. (The names themselves
should not influence your decision.) As with most
investing ideas, there is no one single correct
approach that everyone should follow. I discuss
each of these portfolios in depth in Chapter 6,
and again in Chapter 14. There is also a wealth of
additional information on these portfolios which
you can find simply by searching for them, by
name, on the internet.

Table 5.1

Portfolio Name	Number of Funds	3 Year	5 Year	10 Year
Margarita Portfolio	3	8.00%	2.30%	8.00%
Lazy Three Fund Portfolio	3	10.60%	4.40%	7.70%
Yale U's Unconventional Portfolio	6	10.50%	3.60%	9.10%
Coffeehouse Portfolio	7	9.40%	3.90%	7.90%
Aronson Family Taxable Portfolio	11	9.60%	3.50%	9.40%
S&P 500		10.80%	1.70%	7.00%

As of December 2012

The recommended portfolios noted in Table 5.1 come from a variety of sources. They have been created by investment professionals, including the gentleman who runs the Yale Endowment Fund, investment advisors, stock brokers, and a newspaper columnist. Some of you may notice that these portfolios are created by the same people (the financial advisory community) that I told you to watch out for earlier. However, each of the portfolio options referenced herein have been time-tested and have continually outperformed many other investment options. (Remember, past performance is no guarantee of future results.) I'm certainly not going to suggest that these are the only possible portfolio alternatives, but these portfolios are very logical options for most investors.

Let's take a closer look at Table 5.1 above. The first column lists the names of the recommended passive investing portfolios. The second column lists the number of funds in each of the portfolios. These portfolios range in complexity, starting with two portfolios that have just three funds each (Margarita Portfolio and Lazy Three Fund Portfolio) and increase in complexity down towards the Aronson Family Taxable Portfolio which has 11 different funds. If you choose to invest in any of these portfolios, you will need to divide the money you are investing amongst the number of funds in each portfolio in predetermined proportions. That means that if you select either of the three-fund portfolios, you will need to divide the amount of money you are investing between only three funds, according to the designated proportions of that portfolio; not all funds are given an equal weighting. (I will elaborate on this in Chapter 14.) Contrast that with the Aronson Family Taxable Portfolio with its eleven funds. If you select this portfolio, you would divide the amount of money that you are investing amongst eleven different funds, according to the predetermined proportions. As you continue reading, you'll see that this sounds considerably more complicated than it is.

Maintaining a portfolio with as few as three funds is obviously going to be easier than trying to coordinate a portfolio comprised of eleven different funds. However, additional funds can lower your investment risk by adding greater diversification. (Note: by buying index funds, you are already diversifying your investments since these funds are comprised of a variety of stocks or bonds themselves, thereby reducing your risk. Also each of these portfolios diversifies risk by investing in USA-based stock funds, international [non-USA based] stock funds, and bond funds).

The remaining columns in Table 5.1 indicate how well each of the passive portfolios has performed over various periods of time. For instance, during the three-year period of 2010 through 2012, the returns on each of the portfolios ranged from a high of 10.6% annually for the Lazy Three Fund Portfolio to a low of 8.0% annually for the Margarita Portfolio. Is 8% to 10% a reasonable return? Let's compare these rates of return to two basic benchmarks: a 5-year CD, and the S&P 500. During that same three-year timeframe, a 5-year CD was paying about 2.5% a year and the S&P 500 returned 10.8%. So is 8% or 10% a reasonable return? Absolutely! Our goal as passive investors is to achieve a reasonable rate of return with minimized risk. Each of the recommended port-folios meets this goal.

In the previous paragraph I mentioned annual rate of return. (Annualized returns assume that you are allowing your investment earnings to compound over time.) That 8% return for the basic three-fund Margarita Portfolio mentioned above was an annualized average return. Let me make sure that you understand the concept of an annualized return. Let's assume that you had invested $10,000 into this portfolio three years ago. That 8% annualized return means that this portfolio would now be worth more than $12,597. But wait... shouldn't an 8% return on a $10,000 investment result in a $2,400 gain? After all, 8% of $10,000 is $800, and an $800 gain multiplied by three years would be $2,400, right? Wrong! Don't forget that the gains get compounded annually too. See Table 5.2 below which illustrates the effect of compounding on annual returns.

Table 5.2

Compounding Example	Starting Balance	8% Annual Gain	Ending Balance
1st Year	$10,000.00	$800.00	$10,800.00
2nd Year	$10,800.00	$864.00	$11,664.00
3rd Year	$11,664.00	$933.12	$12,597.12

Let's get back to Table 5.1 now. The bottom row of the table shows the performance of the S&P 500. I have included the S&P 500 merely for comparison purposes. As you can see, during the three-year period ended December 2012, the S&P 500 (by itself) outperformed every one of these recommended portfolios. The S&P 500's recent performance might have you thinking that maybe you should just invest all of your money into an S&P 500 index fund as the S&P 500 has outperformed all of the recommended portfolios over this isolated three-year period of time. While there are people who take this approach to investing, I do not advocate this as a sound passive investment strategy.

Why not simply invest in the S&P 500 rather than a mix of index funds? It is never prudent to put all your eggs in one basket; even if that basket is comprised of 500 of the largest companies in the USA. By investing in an S&P 500 fund alone, you would only be investing in USA-based stocks, not in international stocks (non-USA based companies) and not in bonds, thereby increasing your risk of loss should the United States economy hit a significant bump in the road.

Each of the recommended passive portfolios is mainly comprised of three different baskets: USA-based stocks, international stocks, and bonds. In late 2008, the stock markets (both USA-based stocks and international stocks) lost more than 30% of their value. Since then, these indices have rebounded and erased all of their losses. But what if you needed to take money out of the stock market during that time? You would have done so when prices were declining (for the most part) and the markets were depressed. Therefore, you would have been taking money out of the stock market when the otherwise prudent thing to do would have been to be to investing more. Ideally, you don't want to be forced to sell when the price of your investment is depressed. Assuming you only owned the S&P 500 and needed to sell some of your portfolio for cash, you would have had no other option. Diversifying with international funds and bonds may help minimize this somewhat.

Still not convinced? Yes, the S&P 500 outperformed all of the portfolios listed in Table 5.1 during that three-year timeframe. But how did it perform over longer timeframes? Over a five-year and ten-year timeframe, the S&P 500 has underperformed all of the portfolios listed here.

I'm going to go off on a slight tangent here, but this is a very important point for you to understand. In case you are still tempted by the S&P 500's recent results as reflected in Table 5.1, I'd like to explain why making investment decisions based upon very short timeframes may not be the best course of action. Reviewing the next few charts should illustrate that point clearly.

Chart 5.1 below depicts the daily closing prices for the S&P 500 for the three-year period of January 1, 2010 through December 31, 2012.

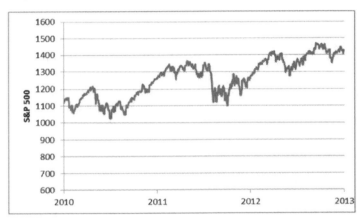

As you can see, there were a few periods of decline in the chart, but there is an overall upward trend. Over this three-year period, the S&P 500 had an annualized gain of about 8.55%. As we just discussed, that is a good return to aim for. However, this reflects a moment in time so to speak. Now let's look at the previous three years, 2007 through 2009 (as illustrated in Chart 5.2). This timeframe includes the period of economic decline due to the difficulties in the housing market and financial sector as a whole.

CHART 5.2

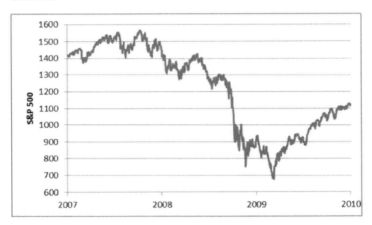

This three-year period shows a marked downward trend through 2008, bottoming out in early 2009, before the market rebounded an erased some of those losses by the end of 2009. Overall, during this three-year period, the S&P 500 suffered an annualized 7.7% decline. I'm sure I don't need to say that this is certainly NOT a return we would aim for! As a prudent investing strategy, we invest a portion of money into bond funds in the hopes of somewhat offsetting these potential declines.

The results are considerably more dramatic when looking at a one-year chart. Chart 5.3 illustrates the S&P 500's performance during the calendar-year 2008.

CHART 5.3

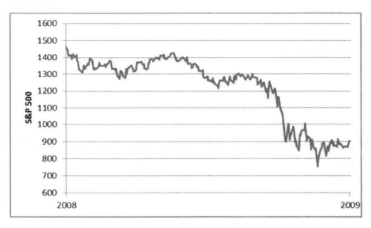

During that one-year period, the S&P 500 lost about 38% of its value. The difference in these three charts illustrates how drawing conclusions based upon short timeframes can dramatically alter your results.

Let's look at a much longer timeframe. Chart 5.4 shows the S&P 500's performance over the 20-year period from 1993 through 2012.

CHART 5.4

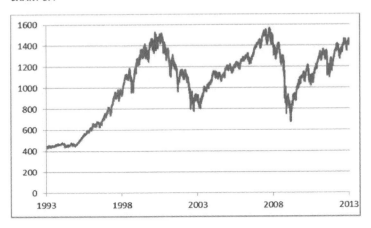

As you can see, there were two periods of significant decline – reflecting both the dot-com bubble in the early 2000's as well as the housing bubble and the downturn in the financial sector in 2008. However, over the longer 20-year period, the S&P 500 experienced a general upward movement and had an annualized return of about 6.1%. During the 30-year period ending in 2012, the value of the S&P 500 increased by about 8.0% annually (not shown on the chart).

The economy and the stock market have grown historically at about an 8% annual rate. Sometimes, however, the stock market suffers from "irrational exuberance" and stock prices soar well beyond their worth. When that happens, invariably there will be a "market correction" and prices will often revert back to normal levels. Sometimes the market might "overcorrect" and "punish" stock prices causing them to plunge. Unfortunately, there is no real effective way for us to predict when any of these events will occur.

Some years the markets go up, and in other years, they decline. As I mentioned earlier, there have been a few years during the recent past when the S&P 500 lost more than 30% of its value. As indicated above in chart 5.3, 2008 was a very difficult time to be invested in the United States stock market; the S&P 500 lost about 38% of its value that year. Had you invested all of your money solely in an S&P 500 index fund, you would have lost 38% of your value in that one year. That's a significant hit; one you want to avoid at all costs if you can. Unfortunately, international stocks lost money that year as well. Investing in bonds often (but not always) minimizes the effect of downturns in the stock market.

Now let's look at one of the recommended portfolios as an example. One of the simplest portfolios recommended in the book is the Lazy Three Fund Portfolio. As the name suggests, it is comprised of just three funds – a USA-based index stock fund, an international stock fund, and a bond fund. During 2008, the two stock funds lost approximately 40% and 46% of their values, respectively. However, the portfolio as a whole lost "only" about 26% of its value due to the fact that a large portion of the portfolio is comprised of bonds. (As a reminder, the S&P 500 index lost 38% that year.) While a 26% loss is still quite significant, it's a far cry from losing 40% or more.

The bond funds in these portfolios help to protect against losses such as those which occurred in 2008, but they can also lower potential gains. In years when the stock markets are increasing, these portfolios might lag the S&P 500 and other indices, but we are willing to accept these limitations in order to temper potential losses. Over the long term, we are looking to have returns that are comparable to the stock indices without the wild swings. As mentioned above all of these portfolios have outperformed the S&P 500 over the 5-year and 10-year periods ending December 2012 even though they had a significant portion of their investments in bonds.

No one can predict the future. As such, it is always advisable to diversify your portfolio to lower your risk of loss. Each of the portfolios listed herein strives to protect against losses by diversifying into international stock funds and bond funds as well as US stock funds. I will discuss the portfolios in the next chapter.

Chapter 6: Background on the Recommended Portfolios

"The individual investor should act consistently as an investor and not as a speculator."

~ Benjamin Graham (American economist and investor; considered to be the father of value investing.)

Below you will find a brief snapshot of each of the portfolios that I introduced in Chapter 5. I'll spell out the details for each of these portfolios as we move through the rest of this book.

Margarita Portfolio

The Margarita Portfolio was developed by Scott Burns. Mr. Burns is a columnist for the Dallas

Morning News, and has been a financial columnist for more than 30 years. According to The Dallas Morning News, Burns currently ranks as one of the five most widely read personal finance writers in the United States. Burns coined the phrase "Couch Potato Portfolio." (You might have heard the terms "Couch Potato Portfolio" and "Lazy Portfolio" before. Both of these refer to passively managed portfolios, like those discussed in this book.)

Over the years, in his newspaper column, Mr. Burns has presented numerous portfolio ideas for his readers to consider. These portfolios range from the very simple to the very complex, with each subsequent portfolio adding one additional investment fund to the mix. His range of portfolios starts with the Margarita Portfolio. The Margarita Portfolio is a basic three-fund portfolio with one-third of your investment in each of: a total USA-based stock index fund, an international stock index fund, and an inflation-protected United States Treasury bond fund. Therefore, the percentage stock/bond distribution for the Margarita Portfolio is 67/33.

Background on the Recommended Portfolios

As mentioned above, Burns offers additional portfolio ideas. Each of his other portfolios begins with the Margarita Portfolio's three funds and adds additional funds. For instance, the next portfolio in his Couch Potato series is entitled "Four Square." He adds an international (non-USA based) bond fund to this portfolio and suggests that you invest an equal amount (or 25%) in the four options. While Four Square and Burns' other portfolios are not recommended herein, you can learn more about these portfolios, if you desire, by searching the internet for "Scott Burns lazy portfolios."

Mr. Burns has also co-authored a book which received critical acclaim, *The Coming Generational Storm: What You Need to Know about America's Economic Future*. Barron's magazine listed it as one of the 25 best books of 2004. Forbes named this book one of the top 10 business books of 2004. It was endorsed by five Nobel laureates. The book warns of a worldwide generational financial crunch and advises investors how to protect themselves from it.

Lazy Three Fund Portfolio

The Lazy Three Fund Portfolio was created by Rick Ferri. Mr. Ferri is a former stock broker. He is the founder of Portfolio Solutions, LLC (portfoliosolutions.com), a low-fee investment advisory firm, where he continues to act as an investment advisor. Portfolio Solutions manages close to $1 billion in separately managed accounts for high net-worth individuals, families, non-profit organizations, and corporate pension plans.

Mr. Ferri has written several investment books. His most recent book *The Power of Passive Investing: More Wealth with Less Work* is available at Amazon.com.

Like Scott Burns' Margarita Portfolio, Rick Ferri's Lazy Three Fund Portfolio also has only three index funds in which to invest. There are two main differences between the Lazy Three Fund Portfolio and the Margarita Portfolio. The Lazy Three Fund Portfolio uses a more broad-based "total" bond fund [4] whereas the Margarita Portfolio uses an inflation-protected bond fund.

The other significant difference between these two portfolios is the distribution of money amongst the index funds. The Lazy Three Fund Portfolio has a higher allocation towards the USA-based stocks and the bond fund, and a lower allocation to the international stock fund, whereas the Margarita Portfolio has an even allocation across its three funds. Overall, Mr. Ferri recommends a 60/40 split between the stock market and the bond market, with a greater concentration in USA-based stocks as opposed to international stocks. The Lazy Three Fund Portfolio recommends a 40% allocation in the USA-based stock fund, a 20% allocation in the international stock fund, and 40% in the bond fund.

---

4   Broad-based "total" bond funds typically include both government and corporate bonds. Inflation-protected bond funds invest in a specific type of USA-based government bond. These bonds are indexed to inflation in order to protect investors from the negative effects of inflation. They are considered to be extremely low risk.

Yale U's Unconventional Portfolio

The Yale University's Unconventional Portfolio was designed by David Swensen. Mr. Swensen is the portfolio manager for the $19 billion Yale Endowment Fund. (This endowment fund is second only to the Harvard Endowment Fund which is $30 billion.) The Yale Endowment Fund has performed extremely well year-after-year. However, most individual investors will never have the opportunity to invest in many of the investment products in which the Yale Endowment Fund is able to invest. Regardless, you can still benefit from Mr. Swensen's investing acumen via his passive portfolio, the Yale U's Unconventional Portfolio, which he designed specifically for individual investors.

The Margarita Portfolio and the Lazy Three Fund Portfolio each have three investment funds. The Yale Fund has six investment funds, including a real estate fund. In fact, the Yale U's Unconventional Portfolio has the highest concentration in real estate of any of the recommended portfolios. Mr. Swensen's portfolio has a percentage split of 50/30/20. That's 50% in the stock market (30% in USA-based stock funds and

20% in international stock funds), 30% in the bond market, and 20% in the real estate market.

In 2005, David Swensen wrote the book, *Unconventional Success: A Fundamental Approach to Personal Investment.* In this book he detailed the rationale behind The Yale U's Unconventional Portfolio, his portfolio recommendation for individual investors, including a detailed explanation as to why individual investors should not try to beat the market. He offers incontrovertible proof that the for-profit mutual-fund industry has consistently failed to help the average investor. He suggests that most people are better off following his suggested six-fund set-it-and-forget-it portfolio.

Coffeehouse Portfolio

The Coffeehouse Portfolio was constructed by Bill Schultheis in 1999. Mr. Schultheis is a former stock broker at Smith Barney. (Smith Barney is now part of Morgan Stanley Smith Barney.) At the height of the dot-com era in the late 1990's, the stock market was nearing its (then) all-time highs, and traditional valuations were being ignored by many investors. Schultheis devised a portfolio which consists of seven funds with a 50/40/10 split. The Coffeehouse Portfolio has 50% in stocks (the 50% is divided evenly amongst five different USA-based and international stock index funds as follows: 10% in each of four USA-based stock funds totaling 40%, and 10% in an international stock fund), 40% in bonds, and 10% in real estate. With just 10% in international stock funds, this recommended portfolio has the smallest concentration of international funds of all the recommend portfolios.

Schultheis' portfolio was met with derision by members of the investing community, many of whom scoffed at his 40% bond allocation. Very few investment advisors were suggesting high bond allocations at that time as stocks were soaring to (then) unchartered heights. But when the dot-com bubble burst and the stock market crashed during the bear market of 2000-2002, the Coffeehouse Portfolio outperformed the S&P 500 index by an astounding 15% in each of those three years.

Schultheis authored a book which instructs readers how to build a portfolio on their own, *The*

Coffeehouse Investor: How to Build Wealth, Ignore Wall Street, and Get On with Your Life.

Aronson Family Taxable Portfolio

This portfolio was conceived by Ted Aronson. Mr. Aronson is the founder of AJO Partners. AJO Partners was founded in 1984. It is an investment management firm which manages more than $22 billion for nearly one hundred institutional investors.

The Aronson Family Taxable Portfolio is the exact portfolio that Mr. Aronson uses to personally manage his own family's taxable investment portfolio. If the founder of an investment firm that manages $21 billion of institutional money thinks it is good enough for his personal portfolio, it may be worth your consideration too.

This portfolio is the most complex of all the recommended portfolios. It is comprised of eleven different funds. It has a 70/30 mix between stocks and bonds. That is, the recommended asset allocation for this portfolio is to put 70% of the investible money into the stock market (40% in USA-based stock funds and 30% in international stock funds) and 30% in the bond market. If you are going to rebalance your portfolio, and I recommend that you do, you will need to take into consideration that rebalancing this portfolio will be more involved than rebalancing the other portfolios listed here as each of the other portfolios have fewer funds than this one does. (I'll go into detail about rebalancing in Chapter 7.)

Besides managing institutional investors, AJO Partners also manages investment portfolios for individual investors. If you are interested in having Mr. Aronson's company manage your money for you, you might want to get in touch with them (by the way, their minimum initial investment is $25 million). If that's above your reach but you'd still like to learn more about AJO Partners' investment approach, you can find them on the web at: ajopartners.com.

Chapter 7: Why Should I Rebalance My Portfolio?

"The four most dangerous words in investing are: 'this time it's different.'"

~ Sir John Templeton (American-born British investor, businessman, and philanthropist)

There have been numerous studies done regarding portfolio design and the allocation of money amongst various investment options. A well-diversified portfolio with reasonable allocation between stocks and bonds has been shown to have more of an impact on your long-term investment returns than any specific stocks or funds that you may actually select. It's not different this time. This is tried-and-true investment advice.

Once you've decided on a portfolio, you will need to rebalance it periodically. To rebalance your portfolio, you simply need to buy or sell enough shares of your investment vehicles so as to adjust the investment levels back to their originally established proportions. Rebalancing your portfolio is another investment management tool which should help your long term returns.

Let's look at what is involved in the rebalancing process. For illustrative purposes, let's assume that you were to select Scott Burns' Margarita Portfolio as your passively managed portfolio. As a reminder, this portfolio has only three components – a USA-based stock fund, an international stock fund, and a bond fund. The investment allocation amongst the three index funds for the Margarita Portfolio is the same, each fund has one-third of the total amount invested. (The investment allocations for all the portfolios can be found in Chapter 14.) So if you had started out with a $6,000 investment in the Margarita Portfolio, you would have invested $2,000 in each of the three funds.

Table 7.1

Fund	Amount	Allocation Percentage
USA-Based Stock Fund	$2,000	33.33%
International Stock Fund	$2,000	33.33%
Bond Fund	$2,000	33.33%
Total	$6,000	100%

Now let's assume some time has passed and during that time both your stock funds (the USA-based stock fund and the international stock fund) have done quite well. Let's assume that the value of each of the three investments is now as follows:

Table 7.2

Fund	Amount	Allocation Percentage
USA-Based Stock Fund	$2,850	38%
International Stock Fund	$2,550	34%
Bond Fund	$2,100	28%
Total	$7,500	100%

The total value of the portfolio has increased from $6,000 to $7,500. However, the gains were mainly in the two stock funds, with the USA-Based Stock Fund increasing in value from $2,000 to $2,850 and the International Stock Fund increasing from $2,000 to $2,550. The increases in the stock funds have far outpaced the increase in the Bond Fund and now our allocation has gotten a little, shall we say, unbalanced. In order to rectify this, we need to get things back to their original allocation – we need to rebalance our portfolio.

In Table 7.1 we saw that our example portfolio started out with $6,000. The value of our portfolio is now worth $7,500 as depicted in Table 7.2. The proper asset allocation for the Margarita Portfolio is to divide the three investments equally. Therefore, we need to divide the current balance of $7,500 and distribute the money appropriately. The proper adjusted allocation for this portfolio would be:

Table 7.3

Fund	Amount	Allocation Percentage
USA-Based Stock Fund	$2,500	33.33%
International Stock Fund	$2,500	33.33%
Bond Fund	$2,500	33.33%
Total	$7,500	100%

What do we need to do in order to rebalance the portfolio? We need to sell some shares of the funds which are over their original allocation percentage and buy some shares of the funds which are below their original allocation percentage. When we rebalance our portfolio, we need to buy or sell enough shares of each investment option so as to rebalance our portfolio back to its original asset allocation. In this particular instance, it would mean selling some stocks from both the USA-Based Stock Fund and the International Stock Fund and using the cash derived from those sales to buy additional shares in the Bond Fund.

The portfolio is now worth $7,500. Our investment allocation is supposed to divide the cash equally amongst the three funds. This means we would need to adjust the balances of each fund so that they each have $2,500.

The two stock funds have more than $2,500. The bond fund has less than $2,500. In order to re-balance this portfolio, we would need to sell $350 worth of shares in our USA-Based Stock Fund, sell $50 worth of shares in our International Stock Fund, and then use those proceeds to purchase $400 worth of additional shares in the Bond Fund, as illustrated in Table 7.4 below.

Table 7.4

Fund	Current Balance	Adjusted Balance	Buy/Sell?
USA-Based Stock Fund	$2,850	$2,500	Sell $350
International Stock Fund	$2,550	$2,500	Sell $50
Bond Fund	$2,100	$2,500	Buy $400
Total	$7,500	$7,500	

Again, the adjustments described in this example are specific to rebalancing Mr. Burns' Margarita Portfolio which only has three funds; and these three funds are held in equal proportions. If you were to select one of the other recommended portfolios, your rebalancing calculations would be different. The rebalancing calculations would be based on the number of funds and the percent allocation of each fund within those portfolios. That means that when it comes time to adjust your portfolio, you will need to:

- determine what the current investment allocations are;

- compare those to the original allocations for the portfolio that you selected;

- determine how much higher or lower the values of the investment allocations are than they should be;

- calculate how much you need to buy or sell for each investment to rebalance the portfolio back to its original intended allocation; and then

- buy or sell the various funds as determined by your rebalancing calculations.

This sounds much more complicated than it really is. Rebalancing is not that difficult. You are simply adjusting the amount of money there is in each of your investment vehicles, if necessary, so that your portfolio consists of the recommended funds in their recommended proportions. If this sounds a bit intimidating for you, or if you would like a reference tool, I have created a rebalancing spreadsheet. It is available at DollarBits.com. (More details at the end of Chapter 9.)

Let me take a moment to discuss the cost involved in executing these rebalancing trades. When you buy or sell stocks, you usually have to pay a commission to the brokerage house for executing the transaction on your behalf. Even if you are using a discount broker, most stock trades will cost you around $10 each (regardless of the number of shares that you buy or sell). However, the commission schedule for mutual funds is a little different than it is for stocks. Many discount brokers will not charge you to buy or sell shares of selected mutual funds. This is especially true with many index funds. More than likely, and depending upon the specific funds which you select and the brokerage house that you choose, buying and selling shares of these funds might not cost you anything at all. This means there may not be any commissions involved when you rebalance your portfolio. (Your brokerage house should have details on the trading costs of mutual funds on their website.)

While there might not be any commissions involved in rebalancing, there could be tax implications. In taxable accounts you may be subject to capital gains taxes and/or losses based upon the rebalancing transactions. Retirement accounts, like 401(k) accounts, IRA's, etc., are non-taxable until you begin drawing from them, which hopefully won't take place until after you reach retirement age, but non-retirement accounts are taxable. However, having to pay taxes on your gains (in my opinion) is not something that you should concern yourself with too much. Consider the taxes that you are paying as a fee for the success of having profitable transactions. You should simply be aware that you may have to pay taxes on your gains. (Your tax preparer will be able to help you with this.) In any event, the taxes are a small percentage relative to the gains, so you are still ahead of the game even if you have to pay taxes. Don't let the idea of paying taxes dissuade you from rebalancing your portfolio. Rebalancing your portfolio is something you should do automatically.

Do you really need to rebalance? Way back in the introduction, I indicated that you could just "set-it-and-forget-it." Well, yes I did say that basically you are setting it and forgetting it... Everyone is responsible for their own investment decisions, but I believe strongly that you should rebalance your portfolio on a regular, periodic basis.

When I was first married, my wife repeatedly questioned the need to rebalance our portfolio. She said things like, "If the stock market is doing so well, why are we taking money out of the stock market and putting it into the (historically lesser-performing) bond market?" Why indeed? There have been numerous studies that have shown that rebalancing your portfolio will, over the long run, improve your investment returns.

After reading some of these studies [5] and other literature, my wife became a rebalancing convert. She was especially happy in 2009 remembering

---

5   If you are interested in learning more about various studies on portfolio rebalancing, search for: Brinson, Hood, and Beebower (1986); Brinson, Singer, and Beebower (1991); Ibbotson and Kaplan (2000); and Davis, Kinniry, and Sheay (2007).

that we had moved a portion of our stock holdings to bonds in 2008 which allowed us to somewhat minimize the negative impact of the dramatic stock market decline that year.

I strongly advocate that you rebalance your portfolio periodically. You could choose to ignore this advice and not rebalance your portfolio, it's your decision. As I mentioned above, there have been numerous studies performed on rebalancing portfolios. The majority of these studies have indicated that rebalancing has a significantly positive impact on your portfolio's long-term performance. Other studies have shown that rebalancing has a minimal impact. The choice to rebalance remains up to you. Regardless of your decision, you should commit to one approach (rebalance or not) and stick with it. Personally, I believe rebalancing is a prudent investing strategy.

So why do I believe in rebalancing since stocks tend to outperform bonds over the long haul? After all, why not just "let the winners run?" There is an expression used by many investors: "pigs get fat; hogs get slaughtered." We want to be pigs, not hogs. Sure it would be nice to become a millionaire overnight, but remember, you cannot predict what might happen tomorrow. There are times when the stock market appears to be in a state of euphoria and stock prices look like they might just climb forever, uninterrupted. That's not the case. Just look back at 2008!

So should you rebalance? We can't successfully time the markets. We will never know the exact right moment at which to buy any particular investment vehicle, and because of that fact, we shouldn't try. (More on market timing in Chapter 9.) By selecting a date to periodically rebalance your portfolio, you can protect some of your gains. When it comes time to rebalance your portfolio, you will need to sell a portion of your "winners" and use the proceeds to buy more shares of those investments whose asset allocations are below their intended percentage. So when the preselected date comes around for you to rebalance your portfolio, if stocks are going up, you get to take some of the gains from the stock funds and invest those profits into your bond fund. Conversely, when it's time for you to rebalance, if the stock market has declined and your stock values are lower, you then take some of that "safe" money from the bond fund and move it into the stock funds. (As a reminder, as passive investors we are investing in index funds, not individual stocks and bonds.) Remember the "pigs get fat" expression? Basically, we don't want to be greedy hogs. Rebalancing allows us to take our gains from the stock funds and reallocate them into safer bond funds or use the proceeds from the safe bond funds to buy more stocks when prices are relatively low. This reallocation of our money helps minimize the risk of getting figuratively slaughtered as hogs if/when the stock market declines dramatically.

To borrow from Aesop's Fables, sometimes it's the tortoise that wins, sometimes it's the hare. Since we can't predict who will win the race, it is prudent to hedge our bets. That's rebalancing in a nutshell... a way to hedge our bets.

I am not the only one who strongly believes in rebalancing; far from it. The Vanguard Group, the world's largest mutual fund company with about $2 trillion invested agrees that periodic rebalancing is vital. In fact, Vanguard suggests that rebalancing your portfolio (or asset allocation as it is more commonly referred to) is the most important decision in the portfolio-construction process.

So how often should you rebalance your portfolio? There have been numerous studies on this topic as well, along with a variety of recommendations as to how often you should rebalance. There are studies that suggest that you should rebalance your portfolio: monthly, quarterly, semi-annually, yearly, and even every two or three years. Some researchers suggest more closely monitoring your portfolio and rebalancing whenever the recommended allocations get too far afield. David Swensen's team at Yale rebalances their Endowment Portfolio every single day! That's a bit much for the average individual investor. How often you rebalance is really up to you. My suggestion is that you pick a timeframe that you are comfortable with and stick with it. For instance, you might want to follow Yale Endowment fund manager David Swensen's suggestion (no, not to rebalance your portfolio every single day). Mr. Swensen suggests that individual investors ought to rebalance their portfolios at least once per year.

Why Should I Rebalance My Portfolio?

Here's an interesting idea for you to consider. If you are only going to rebalance your portfolio once a year, I would suggest holding off a bit. By waiting just a little bit longer than one year (even just one day longer), any taxable gains that you might realize will be treated as long-term capital gains instead of short-term capital gains. As of the publication date of this book, long-term capital gains are taxed at lower rates than short-term capital gains. So by holding on to your profits until they are considered long-term, you will save money on your taxes too. For advice on how this matter affects you specifically, I strongly suggest that you consult with your tax professional.

The following is recommended only for those that want to more-closely monitor their portfolios. As an alternative to rebalancing your portfolio on a predetermined, scheduled date, you might want to rebalance your portfolio when it gets too "unbalanced." Some people choose to adjust their portfolio when the recommended allocations get out of whack. For instance, some people adjust their portfolios back to the recommended allocations whenever any position is 5% or more away from its recommended allocation. So if the allocation for USA-based stocks was recommended at 40%, you might want to rebalance your portfolio when USA-based stocks comprise more than 45% of your portfolio or less than 35% of your portfolio. (While 5% is a reasonable adjustment variance to use, it is not set in stone. You could use any percent variance that you choose.)

As with a predetermined rebalance date, this approach allows you to periodically adjust your portfolio so as to sell a portion of those investments that are exceeding their intended asset allocations and/or buy more shares of those investments whose asset allocations are below their intended percentage. By using a percent allocation rebalancing schedule, you might be rebalancing your portfolio more often than you would be with a scheduled approach. On the other hand, you might actually be rebalancing less often. It all depends on how volatile the markets are.

How often should you monitor your portfolio to see if the allocations are out of whack? Earlier in this book, I mentioned that the folks who run the Yale Endowment Portfolio adjust their allocation on a daily basis. They are essentially rebalancing their portfolio back to its intended allocation every single day. I wouldn't recommend that anyone do that with their own portfolio. So how often should you monitor your portfolio to see if you need to rebalance? Use your own discretion. It could be monthly. It could be quarterly. It could be twice a year. Regardless as to how often you check the current allocation, this approach certainly requires that you pay much more attention to your portfolio than if you were to just rebalance on a regular predetermined schedule. Once again, I would not recommend this for most people. However, I felt that it was important to include this for those of you who want to monitor your portfolios more closely.

Chapter 8: Asset Allocation and Age

"...You have to be constantly reinventing yourself and investing in the future... You're never a finished piece of work. You're always learning new, important things..."

~ Reid Hoffman (co-founder of LinkedIn)

The Vanguard Group suggests that rebalancing your portfolio (or asset allocation) is the most important decision in the portfolio-construction process. I know that I covered this in the previous chapter, but I don't think this point can be stressed enough.

Asset allocation mainly pertains to the distribution of money between investment vehicles. That is, what percent of your money gets allocated to USA-based stocks, what percent is for international stocks, bonds, etc.

Many people believe that your age should be a factor in the asset allocation of your portfolio. This investing philosophy states that as you get older you should allocate a higher proportion of your investment dollars in safer investment vehicles (bonds), thereby decreasing your allocation in theoretically riskier investment vehicles (stocks). This strategy strives to attain wealth early in your investing career, and as you get older, preserve the wealth you have amassed over time.

Each of the portfolios in this book has a suggested asset allocation. These are tried-and-true investment portfolios. They have established, recommended investment allocations. I believe that there is no need to modify these allocations. However, everyone is different. Some investors may wish to tweak the investment allocations in these portfolios to suit their own personal needs and financial situation. Personally, I have not adjusted my asset allocation as I've gotten older, but again, this is a personal decision which you need to make for yourself. Each of us has our own goals and needs. Are you saving for retirement? Do you need the cash sooner than later so as be able to put your children through college? Do you need cash for a down payment to buy a new home? Your specific goals for your money might impact your asset allocation.

Again, I am not advocating that you consider any such modifications to the recommended allocations. However, in the interest of presenting several passive portfolio strategies, here are two additional ideas which you might want to consider when making your personal asset allocation decisions:

IDEA #1: Benjamin Graham, a famous stock market investor thought to be the "father of value investing," believed that the most important asset allocation decision that you will make is the apportionment between risky assets (stocks) and non-risky assets (bonds). He offered some timeless advice: "We have suggested as a fundamental guiding rule that the investor should never have less than 25% or more than 75% of his funds in common stocks, with a consequent inverse range of 75% to 25% in bonds." Obviously, Mr. Graham did not promote altering your asset allocation as you age. He merely suggested that you should invest a portion of your money (between 25% and 75%) in both stocks and bonds.

IDEA #2: John Bogle, founder of the Vanguard Group, recommends investing "roughly your age in bonds."

Following Bogle's recommendation, a 45 year-old should have an asset allocation comprised of 45% in high-quality bonds and 55% in stocks, while a 30 year-old should have an allocation of 30% in bonds and 70% in stocks. This is an example of the age-based allocation I mentioned earlier. There is usually a greater opportunity to grow your money with stocks than with bonds. Conversely, there is a greater risk of significant loss when investing in stocks than bonds. If you experience significant losses as a younger person, the theory is that you have a longer period of time in which to make up for those losses. Bonds tend to be more secure, but offer less potential for growth. As you get closer to retirement age, conventional wisdom dictates that you take fewer risks with your money because you probably need to live on that money during your retirement years, therefore you should own a larger percentage of bonds versus stocks. (Note: We're talking about safe bonds here, like United States Treasury Bonds, municipal bonds, and high-grade corporate bonds, not low-grade "junk bonds.")

Again, each of the recommended passive portfolios has a suggested asset allocation, and in my opinion, there is no need to change those allocations (clearly, I subscribe to Benjamin Graham's philosophy noted above in Idea #1). However, the choice is yours.

Chapter 9: Timing the Market

> *"After nearly 50 years in this business, I do not know of anybody who has done it successfully and consistently. I don't even know of anybody who knows anybody who has done it successfully and consistently."*
>
> *~ John Bogle (founder of the Vanguard Group of mutual funds, speaking on the topic of market timing)*

Timing the market means that you are trying to ascertain the exact right time to buy or sell your investments. We aren't going to try to time the market. Regularly scheduled rebalancing of our portfolios is much more effective than trying to time the market. If you still aren't convinced, go back and reread Chapter 7.

I suggest that you pick a specific date to rebalance your portfolio and adjust your portfolio accordingly. If you decide to rebalance quarterly, you might choose the first Monday of the quarter. If you decide to adjust annually, you might choose the first Monday of every February. (Note: these are random dates chosen for illustrative purposes only. Feel free to choose any date that works for you. You actually might want to set a reminder on your smartphone.)

You may find it a little unsettling the first few times you rebalance your portfolio, especially if there's been significant movement in the markets. If the stock market has gone up considerably you might be thinking, "I've been making a lot of money in stocks, why mess with a good thing?" I went into a lot of detail in Chapter 7 regarding this very issue, but you may still be tempted to try and time the market. You may find yourself thinking, "My current allocation is making me a lot of money; I'll put off the rebalance until next month." But you don't have a crystal ball, and you don't know what will happen tomorrow. Markets can fluctuate, sometimes wildly. By the time "next month" rolls around, the stock market may have moved against you. It may have moved against you significantly. It's not unheard of to have 5% gains or losses in a month. That is why, for most people, I suggest that you establish a pre-determined date to do your rebalancing. We cannot predict the future, and over time, the consistent rebalancing of a portfolio is one of the best ways to insure profitability.

Again, Vanguard suggests that consistent periodic rebalancing is the most important decision in the portfolio-construction process. OK, you probably think I've beaten that point to death. But I'm going to give you one more example.

Let's turn back the clock to March 2009 when the stock market was performing poorly. The financial markets had been in turmoil for several months and the S&P 500 had lost well over 30% during the previous year. Many of us would not have felt comfortable buying stocks when the market was going down and it appeared that "everyone" else was selling their stocks and "putting their money in their mattresses." When it comes time for you to rebalance your portfolio, that scenario might be exactly the one you are faced with. You might find yourself in the position of needing to buy stock funds in order to rebalance your portfolio when the stock market has been falling precipitously.

The same holds true when the stock market is rising. You might need to sell your stock funds when it appears that "everyone" else is buying stocks and driving the prices up. Sometimes it might take a lot of intestinal fortitude to follow through with your rebalancing plan and buy when it seems that all others are selling, or sell when everyone else is buying. Just remember: pigs get fat; hogs get slaughtered...

Act without emotion. Remember what Warren Buffett (one of the most successful investors in history) says, "Be fearful when others are greedy and greedy when others are fearful." When it's time for you to rebalance your portfolio, just do it. You perform regularly scheduled maintenance on your vehicle. You go to the doctor and the dentist for preventative checkups and cleanings. Think of rebalancing as a regularly scheduled maintenance for your investment portfolio. Just do it when it is scheduled!

If doing the necessary calculations to rebalance your portfolio seems a bit too daunting or confusing, or you would just like to save some time, I have created a spreadsheet which will help to streamline the process for you. You simply enter: the names of funds in your portfolio; the recommended asset allocation for each of the funds; and the current value of each of the holdings in your portfolio. The spreadsheet then calculates how much you would need to either buy or sell of each of your funds in order to rebalance the portfolio back to its intended asset allocation. Further instructions are available on the spreadsheet itself.

If you would like a copy of the spreadsheet, it is available for free on my website, DollarBits.com. Simply go to the website and sign up for our updates – there is a sign up box on the upper right hand corner of the website. Once you sign up and confirm your newsletter subscription, you will be taken to a page where you will be able to download the spreadsheet.

Chapter 10: Which Portfolio Should I Select?

> "I guess I should warn you, if I turn out to be particularly clear, you've probably misunderstood what I've said."
>
> ~ Alan Greenspan (American economist who served as Chairman of the Federal Reserve of the United States from 1987 to 2006)

Princeton University Professor Burton G. Malkiel says in his bestselling book, *A Random Walk Down Wall Street*, that "A blindfolded monkey throwing darts at a newspaper's financial pages could select a portfolio that would do just as well as one carefully selected by experts." Could this really be true? Robert Arnett, CEO of Research Associates, indicated while speaking at a conference in late 2012 that Malkiel was wrong. Arnett said, "The monkeys have done a much better job than both the experts and the stock market." [6]

So with a nod to Professor Malkiel, Mr. Arnett, and all of the blindfolded monkeys, which portfolio do I recommend? Well, all of them! I recommend that you choose a passive investing portfolio, set a date to rebalance your portfolio, assess your personal financial situation and goals to determine if any modifications are necessary, and stick with your plan. It's that simple. It's up to you to select the portfolio that's right for you, based on your own research and comfort level. The passive investing portfolios recommended in this book all have a proven record of working well for almost everyone. Remember, whichever investment strategy you choose -- whether it's one of the passive investing portfolios in this book or something else entirely -- the most important thing you need to do is to rebalance your portfolio on a regular basis.

---

6 An article written by Rick Ferris in Forbes in December 2012. (As a reminder, Mr. Ferris is the creator of one of our recommended portfolios.)

As a reminder, you need to consider the complexities involved in rebalancing your portfolio. If you select a portfolio that has eleven funds, you will have to adjust some or possibly all of those eleven funds to rebalance your allocation back to the appropriate, recommended levels. This could mean that you may need to buy and sell shares in as many as eleven funds. For some people, performing this action, even just once a year or so, may be too daunting. If that describes you, then you might want to opt for one of the portfolios with fewer funds.

Some people will feel more comfortable with fewer funds when it comes time to rebalance their portfolio, whereas other people will feel more comfortable with a larger mix of funds, enabling them to spread the risk around more. I have presented several recommended portfolios for you to choose from. These are not the only possibilities. There are many more passive portfolios out there. You can use one of the recommended portfolios in this book, or you can search out other portfolio options.

When it comes time to constructing your portfolio, you might want to tweak the allocation between the various asset classes based upon your age and/or your personal goals and aspirations. If you are a more sophisticated investor, you may even want to create your own portfolio. You can do so merely by altering the percentage allocation for the various funds or adding or subtracting some of the fund options. I will go into this a bit further in the next chapter. Unless you are prepared to do considerable research on your own, I would suggest adhering to one of the preselected model portfolios.

If you are curious, I personally use David Swensen's Yale U's Unconventional Portfolio. I rebalance my portfolio every 370 days AND when any of the recommended asset allocations vary by 5% or more. (Of course, if the market is closed on my rebalancing day because it happens to be a holiday or a weekend day, I rebalance the next day the market is open for trading.) But remember, the ultimate decision about what to invest in and when to rebalance rests with you. Make a plan and stick with it (and don't forget to rebalance). You don't want to change course midstream to go after the latest fad.

Why do I invest this way? My portfolio is well diversified among low-cost index funds which track the markets. That alone allows me to out-perform 80% of the managed funds. I don't have access to superior information. Many investment advisors have access to much more information than I do. They can react to economic news and market changes much more quickly than I can. As such, I shy away from most individual stocks and keep a significant portion of my money in index funds. By doing so, I know that my returns will closely track the stock market and will likely out-perform 80% of the actively managed mutual funds. For the sake of disclosure, not all of my investments are in index funds. I do own individual stocks in my family's portfolio. But as I mentioned earlier, the information in this book is for people who do not have the time, inclination, skills, or the interest to closely monitor the stock market. Clearly, this subject matter is interesting to me.

The recommended portfolios in this book have proven over the long-run that they perform better than many of the other options that are available to most people. However, when looking at the various strategies that are available to you, always remember that past performance is no assurance of future results.

Chapter 11: DIY Portfolio Design

"... as a bull market continues, almost anything you buy goes up. It makes you feel that investing in stocks is very easy and it's very safe and, most important of all, that you're a financial genius... so it induces a dangerous feeling of invincibility..."

~ Ron Chernow (American writer, journalist, historian, and biographer of business, finance, and American politics)

I feel that the portfolios that are included in this book are reasonable, sound, and appropriate for most people. However, I am sure that there are some of you who would like to design and construct your own portfolio. If you intend to be a

DIY ("Do It Yourself") Portfolio Designer, the recommended portfolios in this book offer a good starting point. For those of you with no interest in creating your own portfolio, feel free to skip ahead to the next chapter.

Once again for the sake of simplicity, let's use Mr. Burns' Margarita Portfolio as our starting point for DIY portfolio construction. As a refresher, this portfolio has only three components – a USA-based stock fund, an international stock fund, and a bond fund. The allocation for these three funds is essentially the same; you would invest one third of your investment dollars into each of them.

If you are going to build your own portfolio and you are wondering what types of modifications you could make to Mr. Burns' basic three-fund portfolio, here are a few ideas. Perhaps you believe that the United States economy is on the decline and you want to invest more of your money in international stocks than in USA-based stocks. To do this, you would simply adjust the initial allocation. So, for instance, you could have an allocation of 30/40/30 with a 40% investment in the international stock fund, a 30% investment in a USA-based stock fund, and a 30% investment in the bond fund.

As discussed in the chapter on asset allocation (Chapter 8), you might want to adjust the asset allocation based on your age. Many people believe that as you get older, you should have a lower allocation invested in stocks and a higher allocation invested in bonds. So you might stick with Burns' 33/33/33 allocation when you are in your 30's, and then adjust the allocation as you get older. Perhaps when you turn 40 years old, you would increase you bond allocation to 40%, so your allocation would be 30/30/40. Then, when you turn 50, you might adjust your allocation to 25/25/50. Maybe you want to modify your asset allocation more often than once every decade. Maybe you may want to adjust your age-based allocation every single year. So, for example, when you turn 38 your allocation might be 31/31/38. When you turn 39 you might then want to adjust your allocation to 30.5/30.5/39. You get the idea...

You don't have to use the Margarita Portfolio as your starting point. (I have used it throughout because it is a very basic example, and more easily understood by the casual reader.) You could use any of the recommended portfolios for these types of adjustments; remember however, as you add more funds, the investment allocation and rebalancing becomes a bit more complicated.

There are many people who just use a three-pronged approach to their portfolio. If you are interested in learning more about this, you can read more about it on the internet: http://bogleheads.org /wiki/Three-fund_portfolio.

Once again, I do not generally recommend the idea of creating your own portfolio. I think that any one of the five recommended portfolios presented in this book would be a reasonable and appropriate option for most people. However if you are a DIY sort of person, or if you have a bit of investing experience and knowledge, you may want to consider some sort of adjustment to the allocations.

Chapter 12: When Should I Invest?

> *"Learn every day, but especially from the experiences of others. It's cheaper!"*
>
> ~ *John Bogle*

Once again, using our friend Mr. Burns' Margarita Portfolio as our example, let's take a closer look at investing your money. As a reminder, this portfolio consists of just three funds, a USA-based stock fund, an international stock fund, and a bond fund, in equal proportions.

So let's say that you selected this portfolio and were starting out with $3,000 to invest. You would simply invest $1,000 in each of the three funds. That's fine for your initial investment, but what about subsequent investments? Let's assume that you were going to invest an additional $300 every single month. How would you allocate those new funds?

You have several options: you could invest equal amounts into each fund (in this case $100 each); you could rebalance "on the fly" and invest more into the lesser-performing funds each month; you could let the cash build up in your brokerage account and invest it during your regularly scheduled rebalancing. There is no hard-and-fast rule. Do whatever works for you. Just strive to be consistent.

Generally, the easiest and least painful way to invest is to have the money directly deposited into your brokerage account from your paycheck at work. You may not be aware of this, but many employers offer direct deposit into multiple accounts, so you can apportion your investment money directly into your brokerage account without having to write a check or transfer money.

Some employers will only allow you to deposit money into one account at each financial institution. If that describes your situation, then simply deposit the money into your money market account at your brokerage house and then invest that money either: immediately, during your next portfolio rebalance, or whenever you deem appropriate. (Every brokerage house has one or more money market funds available allowing you to "park" your cash there.)

Alternatively, some direct deposit programs allow you to deposit money into multiple accounts at each financial institution. If that situation applies to you, you might choose to make deposits directly into each of the investment options in your portfolio. Once you have this direct deposit option set up (provided it is available to you) you are then able to invest automatically! For more information on the direct deposit options available to you, consult the HR department where you work.

Investing a similar amount of money on a frequent, regular basis allows you to "dollar cost average" your investments. Dollar cost averaging (DCA) means that you are investing money on a regularly established schedule, without any regard as to how the stock market is doing.

Sometimes when you make your investment, the price of your selected fund will be down and as a result your money will be purchasing more shares of that fund than it would during those times when the price of your fund is up. When the price is up, your invested money will purchase fewer shares with the same dollar amount. If you are investing in your company's 401(k) plan, you are already dollar cost averaging – making a series of small regular investments over a period of time, because you are buying additional shares of your investments each time you get paid by your employer.

Does dollar cost averaging offer better results than investing your money in one lump sum? There have been numerous studies performed on this topic as well. The Vanguard Group performed extensive research comparing returns. They compared the results of a lump sum investment against regular DCA investments over a 12-month period. For their testing, they used a portfolio which consisted of 60% stocks and 40% bonds. Perhaps somewhat surprisingly, the lump sum strategy came out ahead about 67% of the time. The average difference was 2.3%. That is, after running the tests over many different time periods, the portfolio which used the lump sum investing approach ended up with 2.3% more money than the DCA portfolio.

So does this mean that you should save up your money and invest it in one lump sum at a particular time each year? Vanguard's study [7] would suggest that. However I believe that for most people, DCA is the more prudent approach. Even though DCA underperformed lump sum investing, I believe that many people would be much better off using a DCA approach – especially via payroll deductions. The reasons are two-fold. First, I believe that if people were to make one lump sum investment each year, they would try to find the optimum time to invest their money; they would try to time the market. Remember, as we learned in Chapter 9, you can't time the market.

The second reason is ease. If you invest via regular payroll deductions, the process is automatic and essentially invisible to you. You would be investing money without even thinking about it.

---

7 https://pressroom.vanguard.com/nonindexed/7.23.2012_Dollar-cost_ Averaging.pdf

Instead, if you were to have to amass the cash over a year's time and then make a lump sum investment, there is a high likelihood that you might spend at least some of that money or you might actually forget to make your annual investment. So even though the Vanguard study found that the DCA results weren't nearly as good as lump sum investing, I believe that most people would be better offer using the DCA approach.

How much should you invest? That's a personal decision, but my recommendation would be to invest early and often! I strongly believe that you should invest as much as you can. After all, you are saving for your retirement (or your child's tuition, or a new home, or some other long-term goal). The more you save today, the more you'll likely have tomorrow, especially because of the magic of compounding (which I touched on in Chapter 5).

So how much should you invest? Well, I'd recommend investing as much as you reasonably can. But again, that's a personal decision. Let's assume that you are 25 years old and let's assume that our passive portfolio returns 8% annually. If you invest $300 every single month, by the time your turn 65 years old, you would have invested $144,000, but your investment would be worth over $1,000,000! If you are 40 years old and have saved $100,000 to use as an initial investment, and then you continued to invest $300 every month, you too would have nearly $1,000,000 when you turned 65 years old. As you start earning more money, you should strive to invest more each month. Of course, you do not need to invest $300 each month. I am just using that as an example. As I mentioned earlier, how much you invest is a personal decision. However, I strongly recommend that you invest as much as you can.

Chapter 13: How Much Do I Need to Start Investing?

"The investor's chief problem - and even his worst enemy is likely to be himself."

~ Peter Lynch

How much you do you need to start investing using a passive investment strategy? The answer is: that depends. If you are using one of the passive investing strategies recommended in this book, the minimum investment is $1,000. There are a few variables involved in determining the amount you will need to invest, including which brokerage house you use, what type of account you are investing in (retirement or regular), and which portfolio you select.

The brokerage house that you select may have a minimum account size. If you are establishing a retirement account (i.e. an IRA account), many brokers require that you establish the account with $1,000. If you are establishing a regular (retail) brokerage account, most brokers require between $1,000 and $5,000 as their minimum opening balance for an account. You will need to check with your brokerage house to see what their account minimums are. This information is easily found online.

Along with a minimum to establish your brokerage account, many of the index funds that you will purchase have a minimum investment requirement as well. For instance, retail brokerage accounts at The Vanguard Group require a $3,000 minimum per index fund. Fidelity Investments has similar requirements; they require $2,500 per index fund. Again, the initial deposits required to open an account and the index fund minimums vary from broker to broker, and from fund to fund, so check with your brokerage house for their requirements. There are options available for those who choose to invest less.

As I mentioned, Vanguard and Fidelity have minimum funding requirements in their retail accounts for their index funds of $3,000 and $2,500, respectively. These minimum requirements are per index fund. The recommended portfolios in this book each have between three and eleven funds. Therefore, an eleven fund portfolio would require an initial investment of about $30,000 to establish, and a three-fund portfolio would require a $9,000 investment at Vanguard or a $7,500 investment at Fidelity. This may well be beyond many people's means, especially those who are just starting out; or this might not appeal to those who wish to try this strategy with a smaller amount of money.

If you don't have that much money to invest, or wish to invest a smaller amount, there is an excellent alternative. The Charles Schwab brokerage house will allow you to establish an account with as little as $1,000. Further, the minimum initial deposit for the recommended funds in both of the three-fund portfolios is just $100 per fund! This means you can still get started with your passive investment portfolio with as little as $1,000. We'll get into this in greater detail in the next chapter.

Chapter 14: Where to Invest?

"Everyone has the brainpower to make money in stocks. Not everyone has the stomach. If you are susceptible to selling everything in a panic, you ought to avoid stocks and mutual funds altogether."

~ Peter Lynch

Later in this chapter I'll get into the specifics of the recommended portfolios. But first, let's talk about where to invest. Your choice might depend on how much you are going to invest. As mentioned in the previous chapter, the minimum needed to get started with any of the recommended portfolios at Vanguard or Fidelity is $9,000 and $7,500, respectively. If you are planning to invest $7,500 or more, these brokerage houses are established, reputable firms and I recommend them both. However, if you are just starting out, or you don't choose to invest that much money at this time, Charles Schwab has significantly lower minimum requirements. You can establish an account and set up one of the three-fund portfolios for just $1,000 at Schwab. Charles Schwab is an excellent option for the three-fund portfolios (especially for those investing a smaller amount). However, this brokerage house may not be appropriate for some of the other recommended portfolios in this book. The reason is that (at the time that this book was published) Schwab did not offer suitable (low-cost) options for a few of the recommended funds in several of the portfolios.

So which brokerage house should you invest with? Any of the major discount brokers, like Fidelity or Vanguard, offer a wide selection of index funds and can provide good customer service. (There are many reputable brokerage houses. I am focusing on Fidelity and Vanguard here as they are two of the largest brokerage houses, and they are both likely to be accessible to most readers.) Fidelity and Vanguard both have extremely low-cost index funds which would be appropriate for any of these passive investing portfolios. Again, the minimums at Vanguard and Fidelity may be higher than at other brokers (like Charles Schwab). Feel free to research and consider other brokerage houses, as you see fit.

A little later in this chapter you will find a detailed listing of each of the recommended portfolios. For each of the recommended portfolios you will find either two or three tables: one for Vanguard, one for Fidelity, and one for Schwab, where applicable. Each table lists the names of all of the funds which comprise that portfolio, the associated index fund ticker symbol,[8] and the recommended percentage allocation for each investment component.

Please note that there are different ticker symbols listed for the recommended funds at Vanguard, Fidelity, and Schwab. The reason for this is that these brokers each have their own in-house family of funds. By investing in their in-house funds, you will usually be able to avoid any commissions

---

8   A ticker symbol is an abbreviation which is used to uniquely identify all publicly traded stocks and funds.

when you buy and sell initially, when you purchase additional shares, and when you rebalance. If you were to invest on a frequent basis (i.e. every pay period) and had to pay commissions each time you invested, those commissions would significantly, adversely impact your investments. Imagine investing $100 per pay period in each of three index funds and having to pay a $10 commission for each trade. That $30 commission fee would be a 10% expense on each and every purchase! We want to avoid those kinds of expenses wherever possible, so I advocate investing in in-house index funds if your brokerage house offers them. As of the publication date of this book, all of the funds referenced in this book are available without having to pay any commissions. I strongly recommend that you verify this with your brokerage house before making any investment decisions.

Before presenting a detailed listing of each of the recommended portfolios, here are a couple of caveats.

Caveat #1: Please note that some of the funds in three of our recommended portfolios are not index funds. Yes, odd as it might sound after hearing me strongly suggest that you should only invest in index funds, there are a few funds listed here that are actively managed. I continue to recommend all of these portfolios because they stand the test of time, continue to perform well, and because they are very easy to manage.

The Margarita, Yale U's Unconventional, and the Aronson Family Taxable portfolios were all developed with inflation-protected managed funds. (The Aronson Family Taxable Portfolio also includes additional managed funds.) When they were developed, inflation-protected index funds were not available, but now they are. Consequently, all three of these portfolios are being presented with the newly available index funds, however I also present the original inflation-protected managed funds in the notes. For this particular index fund the minimum purchase is $10,000 at Vanguard, and $2,500 at Fidelity. If you select one of these portfolio options, you may choose to invest in either the index fund option, or the original managed fund. I recommend that you use the index fund instead of the actively managed fund, however the $10,000 minimum required to establish a position in this fund at Vanguard may be more than you would like to invest. In that case, I would recommend using the actively managed fund as its minimum is $3,000.

While I have repeatedly suggested avoiding managed funds, you should consider the following points. These recommended portfolios are tried-and-true options that have consistently performed quite well over the long haul, even with a sprinkling of actively managed funds. In the portfolio tables below, you will find a note (letter "A") next to each of the funds that is actively managed. As a reminder, the Yale Endowment Fund Chief Investment Officer, David Swensen, is a strong proponent of index fund-based passive investing and a critic of the mutual fund industry as a whole. Despite that, when he designed Yale U's Unconventional Portfolio, he included an inflation-protected bond fund with the understanding that there was no index fund available at that time. So even though there was no index fund available for an inflation-protected bond fund, Mr. Swensen still included this type of fund in his portfolio. (As noted above, there is an inflation-protected bond index fund available today.)

If buying an actively managed fund is completely unacceptable to you, there are basically three choices. You can consider one of the recommended portfolios which is completely index fund based. If you are interested in a particular portfolio, you can select the recommended index fund option as indicated, or (for the Aronson Family Taxable Portfolio) you can check other brokerage houses to see if they offer index funds for all of the portfolio options listed below. A third option would be to DIY your portfolio and construct a portfolio which uses index funds exclusively. Again, the DIY approach should only be considered by experienced investors.

Caveat #2: Table 5.1 summarizes the historical performance for each of the recommended portfolios. The data for that table included actively managed inflation-protected bond funds, not the inflation-protected bond index fund options, since the index fund equivalents did not exist prior to 2012. So while I am recommending that you use the index funds, I wanted to mention that inflation-protected bond index funds weren't used in the back test, simply because they did not yet exist.

As previously indicated, I have included the inflation-protected bond index fund where applicable, not the actively managed fund, in the fund lineups listed below. If you elect to use the actively managed fund, I have included a note (letter "C" for Vanguard and letter "D" for Fidelity) identifying the actively managed inflation-protected funds which are available at these brokerage houses.

Caveat #3: The Aronson Family Taxable Portfolio includes a fund which, at the time this book was published, is closed to new investors. From time-to-time some mutual funds elect to close their doors to new investors. It is unusual for a fund to close, but (clearly) not unheard of. (When funds close their doors to new investors, they typically still allow existing fund participants to continue to contribute new money to the fund.) At the time that this book was published, Vanguard High-Yield Corporate Fund (ticker symbol: VWEHX) was closed to new investors. Also at publication, Vanguard did not offer a reasonable substitute for new investors. If a fund is not available, an alternative should be chosen. Until such time as Vanguard reopens their high-yield bond fund to new investors, their short-term investment grade bond fund (Vanguard Short-Term Investment-Grade Fund [ticker symbol: VFSTX]) is a reasonable substitute. Bear in mind, it is possible that the high-yield fund might never reopen to new investors. So if you are investing with Vanguard, you might need to accept the short-term investment grade bond fund as a permanent alternative, or for those of you who are "DIY-ers," you might look to select an alternate fund on your own. If the fund does reopen its doors to new investors, it is recommended that you sell your shares in the alternative fund, and buy shares in the recommended, newly reopened fund. Again, this is not a common situation.

That's it for the caveats. Let's look at the recommended portfolios:

Margarita Portfolio

Vanguard

Investment Fund	Ticker Symbol	Allocation
Vanguard Total Stock Market Index Fund	VTSMX	33%
Vanguard Total International Stock Index Fund	VGTSX	33%
Vanguard Short-Term Inflation-Protected Securities Index Fund	VTAPX [C]	33%

Fidelity

Investment Fund	Ticker Symbol	Allocation
Spartan® Total Market Index Fund	FSTMX	33%
Spartan® International Index Fund	FSIIX	33%
Spartan® Inflation-Protected Bond Index Fund	FSIQX [D]	33%

Schwab

Investment Fund	Ticker Symbol	Allocation
Schwab Total Stock Market Index Fund	SWTSX	33%
Schwab International Index Fund	SWISX	33%
Schwab Treasury Inflation-Protected Securities Index Fund	SWRSX	33%

Lazy Three Fund Portfolio

Vanguard

Investment Fund	Ticker Symbol	Allocation
Vanguard Total Stock Market Index Fund	VTSMX	40%
Vanguard Total International Stock Index Fund	VGTSX	20%
Vanguard Total Bond Market Index Fund	VBMFX	40%

Fidelity

Investment Fund	Ticker Symbol	Allocation
Spartan® Total Market Index Fund	FSTMX	40%
Spartan® International Index Fund	FSIIX	20%
Spartan® U.S. Bond Index Fund	FBIDX	40%

Schwab

Investment Fund	Ticker Symbol	Allocation
Schwab Total Stock Market Index Fund	SWTSX	40%
Schwab International Index Fund	SWISX	20%
Schwab Total Bond Market Fund	SWLBX	40%

Yale U's Unconventional Portfolio

Vanguard

Investment Fund	Ticker Symbol	Allocation
Vanguard Total Stock Market Index Fund	VTSMX	30%
Vanguard REIT Index Fund	VGTSX	20%
Vanguard Developed Markets Index Fund	VDMIX	15%
Vanguard Short-Term Inflation-Protected Securities Index Fund	VTAPX [C]	15%
Vanguard Long-Term Treasury Fund	VUSTX [A]	15%
Vanguard Emerging Markets Stock Index Fund	VEIEX	5%

Fidelity

Investment Fund	Ticker Symbol	Allocation
Spartan® Total Market Index Fund	FSTMX	30%
Spartan® Real Estate Index Fund	FRXIX	20%
Spartan® International Index Fund	FSIIX	15%
Spartan® Inflation-Protected Bond Index Fund	FSIQX [D]	15%
Spartan® Long-Term Treasury Bond Index Fund	FLBIX	15%
Spartan® Emerging Markets Index Fund	FPEMX	5%

Coffeehouse Portfolio

Vanguard

Investment Fund	Ticker Symbol	Allocation
Vanguard Total Bond Market Index Fund	VBMFX	40%
Vanguard REIT Index Fund	VGSIX	10%
Vanguard 500 Index Fund	VFINX	10%
Vanguard Small-Cap Index Fund	NAESX	10%
Vanguard Small-Cap Value Index Fund	VISVX	10%
Vanguard Total International Stock Index Fund	VGTSX	10%
Vanguard Value Index Fund	VIVAX	10%

Fidelity

Investment Fund	Ticker Symbol	Allocation
Spartan® U.S. Bond Index Fund	FBIDX	40%
Spartan® Real Estate Index Fund	FRXIX	10%
Spartan® 500 Index Fund	FUSEX	10%
Spartan® Small Cap Index Fund	FSSPX	10%
Rydex Series S&P MidCap 400 Pure Value Fund Class H	RYAVX	10%
Spartan® International Index Fund	FSIIX	10%
Fidelity® Large Cap Value Enhanced Index Fund	FLVEX	10%

Aronson Family Taxable Portfolio

Vanguard

Investment Fund	Ticker Symbol	Allocation
Vanguard Short-Term Inflation-Protected Securities Index Fund	VTAPX [C]	15%
Vanguard Pacific Stock Index Fund	VPACX	15%
Vanguard 500 Index Fund	VFINX	15%
Vanguard Emerging Markets Stock Index Fund	VEIEX	10%
Vanguard Extended Market Index Fund	VEXMX	10%
Vanguard Long-Term Treasury Bond Index Fund	VBLTX	10%
Vanguard European Stock Index Fund	VEURX	5%
Vanguard High-Yield Corporate Fund	VWEHX [B]	5%
Vanguard Small-Cap Growth Index Fund	VISGX	5%
Vanguard Small-Cap Index Fund	NAESX	5%
Vanguard Total Stock Market Index Fund	VTSMX	5%

Fidelity

Investment Fund	Ticker Symbol	Allocation
Spartan® Inflation-Protected Bond Index Fund	FSIQX [D]	15%
Fidelity® Pacific Basin Fund	FPBFX [A]	15%
Spartan® 500 Index Fund	FUSEX	15%
Spartan® Emerging Markets Index Fund	FPEMX	10%
Spartan® Extended Market Index Fund	FSEMX	10%
Spartan® Long-Term Treasury Bond Index Fund	FLBIX	10%
Fidelity® Europe Fund	FIEUX [A]	5%
Fidelity® High Income Fund	SPHIX [A]	5%
Spartan® Small Cap Index Fund	FSSPX	5%
Rydex Series S&P MidCap 400 Pure Value Fund Class H	RYAVX	5%
Spartan® Total Market Index Fund	FSTMX	5%

Portfolio Fund Notes

A. These funds are not index funds, but closely ad-
    here to either their index benchmark and/or are
    the only reasonable alternatives which were
    available at the time of this book's publication.

B. As of the publication date of this book, the
    Vanguard High-Yield Corporate Fund (Ticker
    Symbol: VWEHX) is closed to new investors. Until
    such time that this fund reopens to new investors,
    my suggestion is to use the Vanguard Short-Term
    Investment-Grade Fund (ticker symbol: VFSTX) as
    a substitute. Note: Both these funds are managed
    funds.

C. As a reminder, the Vanguard Short-Term
    Inflation-Protected Securities Index Fund (ticker
    symbol: VTAPX) is the index fund offered in place
    of the original managed fund – the Vanguard
    Inflation-Protected Securities Fund (ticker symbol:
    VIPSX). The original fund was used in calculating
    the historical data in Table 5.1.

D. Note that the Spartan® Inflation-Protected Bond
    Index Fund (ticker symbol: FSIQX) is the index
    fund offered in place of the original managed fund
    – the Fidelity® Inflation-Protected Bond Fund

(ticker symbol: FINPX). The original fund was used in calculating the historical data in Table 5.1.

Once again, all of these portfolios can be used as they are, or customized if you desire. If you are going to create a customized portfolio, you can use any of these portfolios as a starting point to create your own individualized portfolio.

Chapter 15: It's Good to Be Passive Redux

"We have long felt that the only value of stock forecasters is to make fortune-tellers look good... I continue to believe that short-term market forecasts are poison and should be kept locked up in a safe place, away from children and also from grown-ups who behave in the market like children."

~ Warren Buffett

It is important to once again mention that past performance is no guarantee of future results. However, there is a very long history and track record which supports the passive investing strategy.

In my opinion, most people would be better off using a passive investing strategy like one of those mentioned in this book. I believe that most people should avoid all the noise and not buy into the latest fads or chase those hot stocks that are purported to be the next big thing. I also strongly suggest that investors not try to time the stock market.

Basically, unless you are prepared to do a significant amount of research on your own, you should pick one of the recommended passive portfolios listed in this book or find one that you like. The portfolios that are listed here have, over the long haul, consistently performed well.

My suggestion is that you make a plan and stick with it:

- **SELECT A PORTFOLIO**: Select a passive investing portfolio comprised of a small group of index mutual funds to invest in. I suggest that you choose one from the portfolios recommended in Chapter 5.

- **ASSET ALLOCATION**: Determine an asset allocation that's right for you based upon your personal situation. While I recommend that you stick with the original allocations, some people might wish to adjust these allocations as discussed in depth in Chapters 8 and 11.

- **REBALANCE**: Establish a preset time when you will rebalance your portfolio and then do it when that time rolls around, each and every time it rolls around. I suggest that you rebalance every year (plus one day). Do not allow yourself to be influenced by the current economic climate. Don't be afraid to buy when others are selling or sell when others are buying. When it comes times to rebalance your portfolio, just do it!

Good luck and good investing.

Recommended Reading

If you are interested in learning more about investing, especially passive investing strategies, here is a list of books that I recommend.

General Investing Books

- *A Beginner's Guide to Investing* by Ivy Bates and Alex Fry

- *The Neatest Little Guide to Stock Market Investing* by Jason Kelly

- *The Intelligent Investor* by Benjamin Graham

- *A Random Walk Down Wall Street* by Burton G. Malkiel

- *The Little Book of Common Sense Investing* by John C. Bogle

- *The Bogleheads' Guide to Investing* by Taylor Larimore, Mel Lindauer, and Michael LeBoeuf

Asset Allocation Books

- *The Intelligent Asset Allocator* by William Bernstein

- *The Four Pillars of Investing* by William Bernstein

- *All About Asset Allocation* by Richard A. Ferri

Endowment Fund Investing Books

- *Unconventional Success: A Fundamental Approach to Personal Investment* by David F. Swensen

- *The Ivy Portfolio: How to Invest Like the Top Endowments and Avoid Bear Markets* by Mebane T. Faber and Eric W. Richardson

"For Dummies" Investing Series of Books

- *Investing For Dummies* by Eric Tyson

- *Mutual Fund Investing For Dummies* by Eric Tyson

- *Stock Investing For Dummies* by Paul Mladjenovic

- *Investing In Your 20's and 30's For Dummies* by Eric Tyson

- *Personal Finance For Dummies* by Eric Tyson

Additional resources are available at the website DollarBits.com.

Thank You

Thank you very much for buying this book. I hope that you are able to take the information presented herein and put it to good use.

Let others know if you found this book helpful or informative by reviewing it on Amazon.com.

Again, thank you for reading this book.

Good luck and good investing!

About the Author

Who Am I?

Let me start by stating that I am NOT a professional investment advisor nor am I a professional financial advisor. I spent the vast majority of my professional career as a Chief Financial Officer in the private sector. As CFO, I was responsible for the 401(k) administration at my company. That is, it was my responsibility to make certain that the investment options that were made available to hundreds of employees were safe, sound, and appropriate investment products.

For many decades I have been an avid investor, researching investment strategies and managing my family's personal investments. Over the years, I have certainly made some investing mistakes, but I have learned from those mistakes. What you have bought here is the result of my many years of investing research and experience. I hope this book serves you well.

.

41551587R00091

Made in the USA
Middletown, DE
16 March 2017